Challenging. Refreshing. Readable. Risky Business made me think and question, and it provided valuable advice from a long time practising professional.

As a generalisation, private sector managers (entrepreneurs) think they know all about 'risks' and risk management while those in the public sector too frequently think risk is all about 'political risk', in short, keeping the Minister happy. As a result they may not be as receptive to advice from risk professionals and even hold a degree of cynicism. As Bryan so clearly demonstrates in Risky Business, it is up to risk professionals to lift their game and this book will guide you well.

– Pat Barrett
Distinguished Honorary Professor & Senior Fellow – ANCAAR
Research School of Accounting, ANU
Auditor-General of Australia 1995-2005

Even as a seasoned Chief Risk Officer I thoroughly enjoyed reading Bryan Whitefield's latest book 'Risky Business – How Successful Organisations Embrace Uncertainty'. In the world today we are dealing with an unprecedented level of complex societal, business and economic systems and it is important to understand key points of connectivity as to the explicit and implicit flow through impacts on our Risk environment and what the velocity and scale of those impacts might be.

Getting a clear understanding as to the dynamic interconnectivity of your inherent Risks in this uncertain environment is just as critical as understanding the actual inherent Risks themselves. Bryan's book will help all levels of risk practitioner and even folk who don't come from a Governance, Risk and Compliance Background start to make sense of this uncertainty and interconnectivity, and in doing so apply a practical lens over the Risk environments that our organisations face.

– Jason Smith, (Acting) CEO - RMIA & RMIA Director

Risk is one side of the value coin and must be integrated to create and preserve success. In Risky Business, Bryan Whitefield provides practical advice for risk practitioners and other business leaders based on his decades of experience, imbued with his deep passion to help people understand how risk management can help them succeed.

– Scott Langford, Group CEO, St George Community Housing

This book needed to be written. In fact it's long overdue. It's a realistic and very accurate account of what risk actually is and where it's going and it is time we had a reference like this which is easy to understand and use and clears up many risk misconceptions.

If you have anything to do with managing risk then Risky Business is a must read!

– David Turner, Managing Director, RiskNZ

In Risky Business Bryan has so cleverly deconstructed risk into what it is, what it's perceived to be and what it should be – driving the success of an organisation, supporting stakeholders with available information to help them make informed decisions, and improving their engagement with partners.

Risky Business is an enlightening read offering key risk principals as a great 'self-check' for those experienced in risk and for new risk practitioners alike, to ensure we don't become a handbrake to happiness in our own roles. Through Bryan's summary of the risk journey he provides thoughtful insights and deep observations, untangling the technical jargon we stumble over today and even subject our colleagues to.

Bryan's approach to sharing his strategies that have worked so successfully for him around risk management, decision making and influence, will maximise opportunities for even the most experienced risk practitioner out there. This book gifts leaders practical ideas, methods and tools to leverage their impact in their unique environments. Thank you Bryan!

– *Andrew Booth, Head of Operational Risk, Cotton On Group*

Risky Business encapsulates all the important aspects of risk management in an easy to read format. It challenges the way risk is presented in organisations emphasising the importance of avoiding the jargon, understanding culture and the role of persuasiveness, all key elements so often neglected. It provides practical information on the development and use of time horizons and risk appetite, presented in a way that is meaningful and understandable.

Too often risk is seen from a compliance perspective

and presented in a way that reinforces this mindset – perceived as the handbrake in the business, whereas Risky Business focuses on managing uncertainty to drive better outcomes. All organisations need to embrace uncertainty and pursue risk through better risk-based decision making.

Risky Business presents what can sometimes be seen as quite uninspiring topics in a refreshing and inspiring way. It is a book that should be read by anyone who has an interest in, or should have an interest in, how their organisation is managing risk. Bryan has yet again authored a book that distils his wealth of experience and presents it in a format that allows readers to readily apply the knowledge in their own context.

– Valerie King, Executive Director Risk
Uniting Church of Australia Qld Synod (UCAQ)

There is a great opportunity for risk practitioners to increase their ability to positively contribute to the organisations they serve. Risky Business is a distillation of Bryan's 30 years of diverse experience. Bryan takes the reader through a range of relevant content, theories and thinking.

His passion, experiences and examples bring it all to life and together illustrate how we can become trusted advisors and invited to contribute. His book provides an excellent summary of the thinking and tools that can enable risk-based decision making. As Bryan so simply puts it, the goal is to increase the chances of success.

– Grant Gillingham, Group Risk Manager, Fisher & Paykel

A must read for any budding Risk Professional while an excellent reference for anyone in leadership.

> – *Tony Dudley, CFO and Head of Business Enablement Transport Accident Commission*

I have followed Bryan's risk management articles over the years, and these are always very practical and insightful. This book continues the value-add which Bryan so ably conveys.

I could relate to many of the issues and solutions that Bryan has addressed in this latest book. Particular aspects which resonated were in respect to Risk Management Frameworks, Risk Appetite and the building of relationships with Risk Champions (Advocates) across the business.

I would encourage you to take the time to read this book.

> – *Graeme Falloon, Manager Group Risk, Airline Industry*

Risky Business

Other books by the author:

*Persuasive Advising: How to Turn
Red Tape Into Blue Ribbon*

*DECIDE: How to Manage the Risk
in Your Decision Making*

RISKY BUSINESS

HOW SUCCESSFUL ORGANISATIONS EMBRACE UNCERTAINTY

BRYAN WHITEFIELD

Published by Bryan Whitefield Consulting
PO Box 7367 Warringah Mall
Brookvale NSW 2100 Australia

www.bryanwhitefield.com

Copyright © 2021 Bryan Whitefield

Bryan Whitefield asserts the moral right to be identified as the author of this work. First Published October 2020

All rights reserved. No part of this publication may be reproduced, stored in a retrieval system or transmitted in any form or by any means, electronic, mechanical, photocopying, recording or otherwise, without the prior written permission of the publisher.

ISBN 978-0-9945218-3-5

 A catalogue record for this book is available from the National Library of Australia

Cover design by Tim Denmead
Edited by Jem Bates
Typesetting by BookPOD
Printed by IngramSpark

About the author

Bryan Whitefield is a management consultant in the fields of risk, influence and team decision making. His love for solving complexity was fuelled at the start of his career by his studies in chemical engineering, when quite by chance he 'fell into' the field of risk. Since then he has earned a reputation as the go-to guy for demystifying the role and function of risk management in organisations, helping key decision makers value risk management and the risk profession.

Bryan is the author of **DECIDE: How to manage the risk in your decision making** and **Persuasive Advising: How to turn red tape into blue ribbon.** He was President and Chair of the RMIA from 2013 through 2015. Licensed by the RMIA as a Certified Chief Risk Officer (CCRO), he is the designer and, since 2019, facilitator of their flagship Enterprise Risk Management Course. You can learn more about him by visiting www.bryanwhitefield.com.

Acknowledgements

It's funny, the carpenter has a door that does not close quite right, the cobbler has holes in their shoes. Whereas most risk practitioners, me included, practice what we preach. At least so says my number one supporter, the beautiful Jacquie. Darling, thanks for taking a risk on me and coming to Australia from Canada. What a life we have lived, raising three wonderful children into adulthood.

Thanks Doug, Ben and Emily for being true to our family. I love the bonds we all share. And thank you for challenging my parenting as much as you did. It made me a better parent and person by far.

Same goes for you big palukas, my closest friends. You have become a part of me that has provided the resilience to stride through thick and thin while laughing most of the way.

And what of my wonderful support team. The happy, smiley, innovative and always optimistic Paula. And new player in the team, Wendy. The one who has so capably taken on the job of getting inside my head to push me further than I have ever gone before. We make a really great team. We are getting through COVID-19, we will get through and achieve much more. May we be strong together for many more years to come.

To the leaders, faculty and tribe of Thought Leaders Business

School. My career in risk would have been a ho-hum affair without the creativity, discipline and moral support you have given me. And especially you, Dr Pratley, my utmost thanks for your efforts in helping me take on "quantifornication" as I describe in this book.

And what of the RMIA? The Risk Management Institute of Australasia. It has been a big part of my life, as a long-standing member of the NSW Chapter, President of the Chapter, President and Chair of the Board and now a key training partner. I have made many friends over many, many years and I thank you all for being an instrumental part of my risk journey.

Last and by no means least, my clients. My career in risk now spans decades. My consulting practice approaches its twentieth year. I would be dreaming if I believed it had all been rosy. But those who know me well know I love a challenge. Taking on the challenge of making risk relevant, then useful and ultimately valuable has proven a worthy pursuit. One I have thoroughly enjoyed. Thanks to every one of you. Especially those who have become my friends.

P.S. I'm not done yet!

Who should read this book

I have always had a penchant for weighing up the pros and cons of decisions. Maybe it's the boy scout in me, ingrained as a youth with the movement's motto, 'Be Prepared'. Perhaps it was my enjoyment of the sciences at school, where I learned there was more to most things than meets the eye, or perhaps I was just born this way? One thing I'm certain of is that I like to get the most out of life, and to get the most out of life you have to take risks. But you need to take risks with your 'eyes wide open', not when blinded by passion or greed or fear. Doing so, I believe, is the best path to a life without regrets.

Now, I'm no Richard Branson or Elon Musk. They are much, much, much bigger dreamers and doers than I am. Yet I did take a risk when I launched my consulting practice in May 2001 with some money saved, three children under the age of six and my wife Jacquie keeping it all together as a stay-at-home mum. Almost twenty years on, my practice has rolled over the ups and downs of building a business and evolved so that now I have a range of offerings in the fields of risk, influence and team decision making.

Risk is where I have played most and where I have developed a reputation for demystifying the role and function of risk management in organisations in order to teach key decision makers to value risk management and the risk profession.

And what does risk deliver? Nothing less than an increased likelihood of success. Managing risk with eyes wide open means the challenges foreseen are addressed to the best of the organisation's capabilities. It also means that key decision makers are well aware if the organisation's very existence is to be put at risk.

What I have learned about understanding and communicating about risk and risk management is not all contained in this book. The core of it is, though. It is written for risk professionals who want to increase their impact on those they serve, to move from being seen as the Department of 'No!' to the Department of 'Grow!'.

If you are a senior leader in your organisation who cares about extracting the maximum real value from every function in your organisation, read on. Get ready to help the risk function to shift and build on the foundations already in place.

If you are a risk team leader in your organisation, read on. I will help you see some of your challenges and opportunities in a new light.

If you are a member of a risk team, read on. Then please share this with your team so we can all get on with delivering more value!

If you are a front-line worker or in an enabling function,

read on. Improving your ability to manage uncertainty is an increasingly important skill.

And from here on, when I use "you" I am referring to you as a risk adviser, in whatever role performed.

Contents

	Introduction	1
1	**An uncertain world**	5
	The uncertainty paradox	5
	Attributes of successful organisations	7
	Risk management through the decades	12
2	**The drivers of uncertainty**	23
	Complexity	23
	Personal bias	27
	Organisational bias	33
	Is the answer risk management?	35
3	**'Risk' became a dirty word**	39
	Risk vs Risk Management	39
	Risk-speak	41
4	**The agents of complexity**	45
	Complex systems	45
	Agents in a complex system	51
	Influence of regulators	53
	Influence of the 'judges'	56
	Herding the agents	60
5	**The end game**	65
	Beyond resilience	65
	Organisational decision making	70

6	Setting up for success	79
	The thing about risk frameworks	79
	Behaviours	82
	Frameworks	85
	Perceptions	88
7	Designing success	93
	Analysis	93
	Design	99
	Experience	109
	Engagement	112
8	Appetite for business	125
	Does it matter?	125
	What makes it difficult?	129
	Risk appetite framework	133
	Operationalising risk appetite	147
9	Reading the Signals	153
	Signals are the secret to sustainability	153
	KPIs and KRIs	156
	Measures that matter	158
	Developing KRIs	159
	Time horizons	162
	The strategy funnel	164
	Do Black Swans send signals?	167
	Planning in pandemics	170
10	Quantifornication	175
	Plucking numbers out of thin air	175
	The case for good risk assessment	176

	The start of good risk assessment	177
	Analysing risk	180
	Quantifying risk	182
	It's about your data, not big data	192
11	**The pathways to success!**	193
	Risk-based decision making	193
	The pathways	195
12	**Persuasive advising**	203
	Shifting mountains	203
	Shifting values	205
	Shifting gears	207
	The wrap	211
	I am passionate about	211
	Endnotes	213

List of Figures

Figure 1.1:	Risk management through the decades	15
Figure 5.1:	The risk management journey (four phases)	66
Figure 5.2:	The risk management journey (five phases)	70
Figure 6.1:	The thing about risk frameworks	82
Figure 6.2:	Risk leadership means behaviour change	84
Figure 6.3:	The role of frameworks	87
Figure 7.1:	Tripartite Model of Risk Management	103
Figure 7.2:	The Relationship Ladder	117
Figure 7.3:	The three Es of tribe building	123
Figure 8.1:	Risk appetite — aligning the poles	129
Figure 8.2:	Quality of risk appetite statements	133
Figure 8.3:	Risk appetite by role	134
Figure 8.4:	Risk appetite framework	136
Figure 8.5:	Risk maturity healthcheck rating elements	140
Figure 8.6:	Sample decision map	151
Figure 9.1:	Human progress vs time, by Tim Urban, waitbutwhy.com	156
Figure 9.2:	The relationship between strategy and risk over three time horizons	163
Figure 9.3:	The strategy funnel	166
Figure 9.4:	Future Today Institute's action matrix	170
Figure 9.5:	Sample scenarios prepared in June 2020	173
Figure 11.1:	Risk leadership	198
Figure 12.1:	The influence ladder	209

Introduction

I started writing this book in mid-2019 in a pre-COVID-19 world. I was more than halfway through writing it when the pandemic hit. Interestingly, to me at least, nothing fundamental changed in my thinking about risk management. For me it's not rocket science. It's about managing uncertainty. And, done well, it delivers real value for organisations.

> Risk management isn't rocket science. It's about managing uncertainty. And, done well, it delivers real value for organisations.

There are 12 chapters in this book. Chapters 1 through 4 trace the journey the risk profession has taken since the 1990s, when the first national standards for risk management were established. They explore the underlying drivers of risk and the need for risk management. They also point out the failings of the risk profession so far (as teachers would say, 'Must try harder').

Chapters 5 through 7 paint a picture of risk management done well in organisations of larger size, in any country, at any stage of development. I do not cover managing uncertainty in start-ups or small to medium enterprises, although I do note that their greatest strength is their agility and observe that the ultimate aim of risk management in larger organisations is to help them maintain or regain the agility that made them great in the first place. Agility through better decision making.

Chapters 8 through 10 cover specific aspects of risk management: risk appetite, key risk indicators and risk analysis. Here I do not apologise for anything anyone should find controversial. The risk profession needs to be thinking differently if it is to take its rightful seat at the executive table. I have not ventured into the business continuity planning, pandemic planning, or cyber, fraud or capital 'C' Compliance aspects of enterprise risk. I recognise their importance, but also that they are specialties in their own right. Nonetheless, if you are a professional with expertise in one or more of these fields, I'm sure you will gain plenty of insights within these pages on how to do your job better.

> It is one thing to be technically brilliant in the field of risk management; it is altogether another to get others to listen and act on your advice.

Chapter 11 defines what success looks like. And chapter 12 introduces the concept of *persuasive advising*, a core skill that all risk professionals need. It is one thing to be technically brilliant in the field of risk management; it is altogether another to get others to listen and act on your advice.

One final point. Don't be alarmed, but the ultimate risk professional would need an MBA on steroids. To deliver value to the business, you need to *understand* the business. That means you need to understand sales, marketing, production, logistics, finance, people and culture, ICT and every other enabling and delivering function of the business you serve. Tough ask, but that's what is needed if you want to deliver real value.

> Don't be alarmed, but the ultimate risk professional would need an MBA on steroids.

Understand the business and follow the core principles of value-adding enterprise risk management I outline in this book, and you will deliver optimal value for your organisation and will make the impact you aspire to.

1

An uncertain world

The uncertainty paradox

I dislike the term 'VUCA' (an acronym for Volatility, Uncertainty, Complexity and Ambiguity). I don't dislike a world that recognises these attributes — what world does not? I just don't get the term. It feels kind of, well, wrong. A world with volatility, complexity and ambiguity means there is uncertainty. That is, volatility, complexity and ambiguity are drivers of uncertainty. Yes, we need to manage them all but we need to embrace uncertainty.

The reason why organisations need to embrace uncertainty is captured in the Uncertainty Paradox, which states that the only certainty is uncertainty.

> Volatility, complexity and ambiguity are drivers of uncertainty. Yes we need to manage them all but we need to embrace uncertainty.

No one can predict the future. You can't hold your hand on your heart and swear you'll achieve today's goals, let alone the goals you have set for a year or a lifetime. No one knows what's around the corner. No one. There are untold unknowns. What is one of our base fears? Unknowns. And what happens when we fear something? It may be a call to action, or it may trip a fight-or-flight response. We allow our instincts to take over. Other times our mind goes foggy and we freeze. The Uncertainty Paradox demands that we live with uncertainty.

> Sometimes uncertainty generates fear, sometimes it intrigues us: we become inquisitive and investigate the uncertainty, like a scientist, or we become speculative, like a gambler.

Sometimes uncertainty generates fear, sometimes it intrigues us: we become inquisitive and investigate the uncertainty, like a scientist, or we become speculative, like a gambler. Then uncertainty is experienced not as a threat, but as an opportunity. Think of an artist starting a new work of art. They are excited about what they may create, uncertain of how they will realise each element, of how satisfied they will be with the finished work, and of how the work will be perceived by others. Yet they are up for the challenge.

It's the same for organisations. Some kinds of uncertainty generate more fear than others. Uncertainty around the actions of government, a powerful competitor or a disruptive start-up can fog the corporate mind. So much so that many corporations react by doing nothing: they simply wait and see. Like the frog in the pan of heating water. Like Kodak inventing digital camera technology then turning their back on it.

Organisations that embrace uncertainty, on the other hand, follow the creed of *fail often but fail fast*. Think Elon Musk and his SpaceX and Tesla ventures. SpaceX was the first commercial service provider engaged by NASA to take astronauts to the International Space Station. In June 2020 Tesla became the world's most valuable car maker by market capital value. Musk and the big tech companies see uncertainty as opportunity. They are more likely to be disrupter than disrupted.

> Musk and the big tech companies see uncertainty as opportunity. They are more likely to be disrupter than disrupted.

Managing uncertainty is a key to success.

Attributes of successful organisations

Before discussing attributes of successful organisations, it is worth considering what an organisation actually is. Nobel Prize winner Herbert A. Simon may have been the first person to articulate it. In his book *Administrative Behaviour*, published in the 1940s and republished many times since, Simon explains that once the purpose of an organisation is established, all that remains is for management to influence decision making to ensure the most appropriate decisions are made by those within the organisation to fulfil the organisation's purpose. A perfect decision, he proposes, is one in which all possible consequences are foreseen. But there is no such luxury in the real world. Not all consequences are foreseeable. There is always uncertainty.

By default, successful companies are good at managing uncertainty. They are comfortable with it, and the more ambitious of them embrace it. Some do it through traditional sound risk management. Some, like start-ups in the IT sector, embrace it using development methodologies such as Agile. Agile recognises the extreme uncertainty of some technology builds and minimises risk by taking bite-size chunks of a development, one by one, readjusting goals after each chunk. All to fulfil a purpose.

> Adopting sound risk management in an organisation and running an Agile approach to technology development are two ways of embracing uncertainty.

Adopting sound risk management in an organisation and running an Agile approach to technology development are two ways of embracing uncertainty. Both are about getting comfortable with our fears and discomfort. As an analogy to help explain the concept of embracing uncertainty, I describe how the Uncertainty Paradox is applied to treatment of the mental health condition Obsessive Compulsive Disorder (OCD).

OCD is a debilitating condition that can cause high levels of anxiety in individuals. They develop obsessional responses to certain triggers that compel them to act idiosyncratically. According to Jeff Bell, writing in *Psychology Today*, OCD sufferers experience extreme uncertainty, which creates high levels of fear and anxiety.[1] Their obsessions are based on uncertainty — for example around cleanliness, which forces them to clean things again and again. Bell reports that one successful treatment of OCD is a process called exposure and response prevention (ERP), an especially effective form of cognitive behaviour therapy (CBT). He describes it as follows:

> According to Jeff Bell, writing in *Psychology Today*, OCD sufferers experience extreme uncertainty, which creates high levels of fear and anxiety.

'In a nutshell, 'exposure' involves having an OCD client deliberately face a feared situation or object (trigger). And 'response-prevention' involves having that client refrain from the compulsive response that has traditionally brought her temporary relief. To this end, a therapist and client develop a hierarchy of fears, moving from the least anxiety-producing to the most anxiety-producing. With this hierarchical 'ladder' as a guide, the client then learns to systematically face down her fears — and, in so doing, habituates to the discomfort of her anxiety.'

Bell explains that the reason for its effectiveness is habitualisation, a concept described by Tamar Chansky in his book *Freeing Your Child from Obsessive-Compulsive*

Disorder, where he 'likens the process of embracing uncertainty to jumping into a cold swimming pool. At first, the coldness is extremely uncomfortable, and our brains send us messages of "cold, cold, cold" and "Get out! Get out! Get out!" BUT, if we stay in the pool, the water seems to warm up. Of course, it doesn't really get any warmer; instead, we habituate ourselves to the discomfort of the coldness.'

The implication here is that the most successful organisations learn to systematically confront and get comfortable with uncertainty. They learn to embrace it. They face the drivers of their uncertainty, one by one. Those they can proactively manage, they do. When they can't, they put in place a 'Plan B' to manage the fallout if the worst happens. This is the essence of the concept of enterprise risk management. Rather than simply managing what hurt in the past by adding another process over another process, the organisation looks to identify its fears and systematically work through them. It ignores none of them; it lives with each of them and so has a clearer view of them.

> Rather than simply managing what hurt in the past by adding another process over another process, the organisation looks to identify its fears and systematically work through them.

Fortunately, there is increasing empirical evidence of the benefits of a strong enterprise risk management program.

For example, Hoyt and Liebenberg, through a study of publicly listed US insurance companies published in 2015[2]. And Lechner and Gatzert, through a study of publicly listed companies on the German stock exchange published in 2018[3], which found '… a significant positive impact of ERM (enterprise risk management) on shareholder value after controlling for other determinants of firm value'. More recently, Gartner published their findings from research into the success of organisations responding to the COVID-19 pandemic as the crisis evolved in early 2020. In their paper titled *COVID-19 Makes a Strong Business Case for Enterprise Risk Management* they found that 'an agile response occurred far more often when clear processes already existed'.[4] The article also highlighted a problem common to many companies: they treat enterprise risk management as a box-ticking exercise. Those that had done so during the previous decade of strong economic growth either had no Plan B or had plans that did not work

> While Agile principles have their place in all organisations, the focus of this book is on how organisations can best embrace uncertainty through enterprise risk management.

While Agile principles have their place in all organisations, the focus of this book is on how organisations can best embrace uncertainty through enterprise risk management.

Risk management through the decades

Peter Bernstein's great book *Against the Gods: The Remarkable Story of Risk* provides a wondrous history of risk management, from the introduction of the Hindu-Arabic numbering system in the western world in the 1200s to publishing in the 1990s. He ends the book with this most important observation: that the heroes of the story of risk — Pascal, Bernoulli, Knight and Markowitz, to name a few — 'transformed the perception of risk from chance of loss into opportunity for gain, from FATE and ORIGINAL DESIGN to sophisticated, probability-based forecasts of the future, and from helplessness to choice'.[5]

Grand and inspiring words, no doubt, but what of the decades since?

> The world knew things had to change, and the nuclear and chemical industries for example turned to risk management.

The formal management of risk grew strongly in the 1980s and early 1990s. Much of it was driven by both safety and financial concerns. Safety concerns were driven by disasters such as the nuclear meltdown in Chernobyl in the Ukraine, which killed thousands and affected most of Europe, and, two years earlier in 1984, the toxic gas release from a chemical plant in Bhopal, India, owned by Union Carbide of the US, which also killed thousands. On the financial side there was the stock market crash of 1987 and the rogue trader Nick Leeson's destruction of Barings Bank in 1995. The world knew things had to change, and the nuclear and chemical industries for example turned to risk management. New methodologies were developed such as HAZOP (Hazard and Operability Analysis), FMEA (Failure Modes and Effects Analysis) and QRA (Quantitative Risk Assessment).

The new interest in risk management led to the development of the first national standard, AS/NZS 4360 Risk Management, published jointly by Australia and New Zealand in 1995. I had first-hand knowledge of the development of the standard. My boss at the time sat on Risk Management Committee OB7, of Standards Australia and Standards New Zealand. I had the honour of sitting in for him a couple of times in the lead-up to the standard's publication. So I have taken particular interest in its evolution over the decades through variations in 1999, 2004, evolving into the International Standard ISO 31000 in 2009, and its most recent version in 2018. You are probably familiar with the risk management process documented in the standard, so I won't bore you by reproducing it here. I do want to point out one very important augmentation of it, however. The only significant difference between the diagram in AS/NZS 4360 in 1995

> The risk profession knew the beauty of risk management. All that was needed was to put it into a standard and publish it, and the rest of the world would applaud and embrace the process.

> While some organisations, such as those in the mining sector, have dramatically improved safety, other industries have not.

> While some in the finance sector appreciate the advantages of good risk management, others continue to see it as a compliance activity to appease regulators.

and the one in the current ISO standard was that it did not include the 'Communicate and Consult' box. That's right. The risk profession knew the beauty of risk management. All that was needed was to put it into a standard and publish it, and the rest of the world would applaud and embrace the process.

But alas, risk management did not catch on as was hoped. I explain the reasons for this later in the chapter. 'Risk' became a dirty word. While some organisations, such as those in the mining sector, have dramatically improved safety, other industries have not. While some in the finance sector appreciate the advantages of good risk management, others continue to see it as a compliance activity to appease regulators. Looking back over the past few decades (figure 1.1), you can see how enterprise risk management in many organisations floundered and how it has now started to gain traction. Let me help you relive this history and perhaps describe your organisation right now!

Decade	Risk Theme	Business Leadership	Risk Leadership	Value
2020s	Leadership	Be Accountable	Influence	Sustainable Growth
2010s	Insights	Look Forward	Analytics	
2000s	Comfort	Be Prepared	Assurance	Organisational Drag
1990s	Compliance	Tick & Flick	Training	

Figure 1.1: Risk management through the decades

The 1990s: Training to fulfil a compliance need

In the 1990s, as we introduced the risk management standard to organisations across Australia and New Zealand in a nicely complicated way, the most common response from non-risk people was, 'Managing risk is something I do every day. Why do I need to go through this process?'

The result? The risk process became a compliance activity, and the culture of tick and flick was born.

Worse still, it caused serious injury to organisations from which most have never recovered. The responsibility for the risk function was pushed well down in organisations. Rather than a senior executive taking full ownership,

> The risk process became a compliance activity, and the culture of tick and flick was born.

someone was found with time on their hands or with an interest in the topic.

So what did organisations do to be seen to be doing something? They introduced more training of course. The attitude that prevailed among senior management was, 'Well of course our people should be trained to manage risk. After all, that's what I do every day — it's how I got where I am. But please don't bother *me* with the training, and keep all your risk registers to yourself, thanks very much.'

> The attitude that prevailed among senior management was, 'Well of course our people should be trained to manage risk. But please don't bother *me* with the training, and keep all your risk registers to yourself.'

While the training worked for some, for most it failed to shift attitudes.

The 2000s: Assuring to give comfort to someone else

Following major corporate debacles like Barings Bank in the UK, in the 1990s came Enron and Worldcom in the US, FlowTex in Germany, Parmalat in France, and HIH Insurance and OneTel in Australia early in the 2000s. Then we had the GFC around 2008. Through the 'noughties', boards and stakeholders were demanding better management of risk. Better all-round governance, in fact.

The hope of the risk profession was that organisations

would now take risk and its related governance disciplines seriously, as it was an obvious antidote to the problems that marked the decade.

It was not to be. The interpretation of business leaders was that risk was important because the board, and specifically the board's Audit Committee, wanted assurance, often from a regulator, that risk was being managed well. That is, 'We have to do this risk stuff for the comfort of others, not because it adds value to what I do.'

Because the Head of Audit was the Audit Committee's most trusted adviser, more often than not the audit team were given responsibility for the risk management function, and the audit committee became the audit and risk committee, despite the concerns of others that it created a conflict. And their go-to for ideas and resources were of course the large audit firms, the 'Big 4'. Yet more potential conflict of interest to be managed.

> The interpretation of business leaders was that risk was important because the board, and specifically the board's Audit Committee, wanted assurance, often from a regulator, that risk was being managed well.

As the 2000s closed, the assurance industry boomed. That's right. The assurance industry, the industry of getting an audit firm to have a look at the risk process and various areas of compliance to provide assurance to the board that all was well. The result was a culture of 'be prepared, because the auditors are coming', and the attitude that the only reason this stuff needs to be done is to placate the auditors, who need to placate the audit and risk committee. The whole shebang resulted in a lot more red tape.

The 2010s: Analytics to provide insight

As we exit the teenage years of the previous decade, risk management has made good headway in some organisations while others still languish in the 2000s', and some even in the 1990s' approach to risk.

> Those that have strode ahead have developed a forward-looking culture by using analytics to derive strong insights for decision making.

Those that have strode ahead have developed a forward-looking culture by using analytics to derive strong insights for decision making. Industries such as chemicals, finance, mining and retail have led the way. The chemical industry in particular, with the severe consequences of mismanaged complexity, has found more and more means of sophisticated risk modelling supported by a strong risk management culture. By embracing complexity they have maintained their licence to operate and to achieve bigger and bigger goals.

The success of analytics is also highlighted by the finance sector. In Australia, for example, insurance companies are not as vulnerable to collapse as they were in the days of

HIH. Under heavy pressure from the regulator, the industry gained more and more insight into the risk profile of certain products and industry sectors using concepts such as stress testing and scenario analysis. However, analytics alone does not guarantee success. With the growth of AI and machine learning, analytics is being used to gain insight into the culture of organisations. As an example, organisations can now analyse staff emails to detect inappropriate behaviour. Analysis alone does not change behaviour, though. As evidenced by the Financial Services Royal Commission, while the balance sheets of finance sector organisations were much better managed, their conduct left a lot to be desired.

> With the growth of AI and machine learning, analytics is being used to gain insight into the culture of organisations.

The 2020s: Accountability, influence and risk leadership

What of the current decade? We will need the kind of leadership that will ensure organisations are led through an increasingly complex maze. That means a culture in which everyone leans in and takes accountability for risk, rather than outsourcing the management of risk to the risk team or holding up their hands in surrender and saying, 'It's complex, it's hard. Everyone makes mistakes.' It means that the leadership team, assisted by the risk function, applies risk-based decision making to choose when the organisation will take on more risk to seize opportunity, and when to ease back because the risk is not worth taking.

We will need leaders aware of unconscious bias in their own decision making and that of others. Leaders who will put in place the mechanisms to manage their own bias and to challenge those leaders who don't do the same.

> We will need leaders who instil a strong, values-based culture in organisations, who refuse to put short-term profit above sustainable outcomes and who are willing to challenge those who do.

We will need leaders who instil a strong, values-based culture in organisations, who refuse to put short-term profit above sustainable outcomes and who are willing to challenge those who do. These leaders will need to stand up to financial analysts who drive this type of behaviour in leaders of publicly traded companies. And they will need to learn to do so in very compelling ways. In the public sector we will need leaders who can guide ministers more courageously than ever before. No more pink batts or sporting grants scandals caused by the elevation of short-term personal or party gain over the long-term interest of the public.

That means we in the risk profession need to stand up. To become more proficient at delivering value to our clients. To convince leaders to hold themselves accountable to the values of the organisation, to recognise and manage their unconscious bias, to think long term as well as short, and to take account of the insights we bring them. That means we need to convince leaders that what we do is valuable for them.

> Influence, rather than being technically correct, is what changes people's minds and behaviours.

Through the rest of this book I'll share with you what I have learned about overcoming the many challenges facing risk professionals. None of it is especially technical. Most of it is about making risk management as simple and practical as necessary while providing a more than satisfactory level of insight and assurance. I guarantee that this approach is essential to building your influence. And influence, rather than being technically correct, is what changes people's minds and behaviours.

Let's start by looking at the drivers of uncertainty and asking the question, 'Is risk management the answer?'

2

The drivers of uncertainty

Complexity

While volatility, complexity and ambiguity create uncertainty, if you think about it, you will also appreciate that volatility and ambiguity are also drivers of complexity.

I love complexity. I'm fascinated by it. I look at complex things and ask myself, 'How can this be?' or 'WTF?' In fact, I first got into risk because of my fascination with complexity. In my last year of high school my parents were having a dinner party. One of a friend's parents were over. I knew them well, having been to their house many times on sleepovers when I was younger. Barry

> While volatility, complexity and ambiguity create uncertainty, if you think about it, you will also appreciate that volatility and ambiguity are also drivers of complexity.

came over to me and we had the following life-changing conversation:

> Barry: 'What are you thinking of doing next year after school?'
>
> Me: 'Dunno.'
>
> Barry: 'What are you most interested in at school?'
>
> Me: 'Physics, maths, chemistry.'
>
> Barry: 'Have you thought about engineering?'
>
> Me: 'Aurrr!' (Somewhere between a grunt and another dunno.)
>
> Barry: 'You better come to Open Day at Sydney University in a few weeks and have a look around the Faculty of Engineering.'
>
> Me: 'OK.'

So I went to Sydney University for Open Day (sales day at universities in Australia, when they show off their best offerings to prospective students). I met Barry at the Department of Chemical Engineering and he suggested I go see all the other engineering departments first. There was aeronautical, civil, electrical, mechanical and mining, and they really turned it on. Everything that whistled, banged, flashed, shook or otherwise might capture the imagination of their young visitors were on display. And I loved it. I was fascinated.

When I'd completed the circuit I went back to find Barry, who took me on a personal tour of 'Chem Eng', as it was known. He took me into rooms with pipes and monitoring machines, sand beds with gases bubbling up through them, rooms where stuff was being combusted and the gases sampled. All of it was just as fascinating . . . no, more fascinating to me than all the other engineering marvels I had seen that day. Yes, it was the personal tour, but I really loved chemistry at school and worked very hard at it for my final exams. To see what it could lead to in practical terms was wonderful.

> All of it was just as fascinating . . . no, more fascinating to me than all the other engineering marvels I had seen that day.

Then Barry took me into the final lab — a room dominated by a tall glass column separated by steel plates. Liquid was flowing down through holes in the plate while gases were rising up through the same holes. Barry explained that this process was used for separating groups of chemical compounds with different boiling points. He talked on but I barely heard him, staring at the apparatus in wonder.

Then and there I knew I wanted to study Chemical Engineering.

My studies and my career as a chemical engineer and as a fire protection engineer confirmed my first impressions. The industry was complex. How complex? Complex enough for us to build major facilities such as oil rigs, refineries and a host of different types of chemical plants, only to find we did not manage the complexity of them nearly well enough. The broader petrochemical industry killed people and polluted the environment on a frightening scale. Think again of Bhopal in India, or the Piper Alpha oil rig explosion, or the *Exxon Valdez* and Deepwater Horizon environmental disasters.

Around the time I started my career the industry was put on notice by regulators. The message: 'Manage this complexity better or you will lose your licence to operate and/or directors will go to jail.' The industry responded by developing a range of risk management techniques that I mentioned in the previous chapter, such as HAZOP, FMEA and QRA. I learned these techniques and found them powerful tools for helping our already powerful brains to deal with complexity.

> I was in for quite a surprise, because I soon learned that the world of general business was way, way more complex than a petrochemical plant.

By the mid-1990s I was well versed in all these tools and was lucky enough to be in a position to start applying them from the petrochemical and nuclear industries into the world of general business. I was in for quite a surprise, because I soon learned that the world of general business was way, way more complex than a petrochemical plant. Who would have thought?

Why? Because petrochemical plants had a couple of things working in their favour. First there were the irrefutable laws of physics and chemistry. Once a chemical plant was designed and tested, it was safe. Things went wrong only when people got involved. Wanting to change something or to take a short cut on maintenance or to conduct maintenance on the run when the plant was not fully shut down. That's right, science is immutable but people are fallible.

> Science is immutable but people are fallible.

Is there any wonder, then, that in the 2020s an IT project struggles to deliver an application on time and on budget that works pretty much as people want it to work? Even though our IT capabilities are incomparably more advanced than the computers that made possible the first moon landing in 1969? IT projects are infinitely more complex than chemical plants because they involve people at every step of the way. People who can't quite articulate what they want, who change their minds, who try to work around 'the system'.

And of course, we people are fooled by the unconscious biases that affect our decision making.

Personal bias

Our personal and, most importantly, *unconscious* biases are a curse that time and time again causes us to make less than optimal decisions. While

> Our personal and, most importantly, *unconscious* biases are a curse that time and time again causes us to make less than optimal decisions.

sometimes this leads to unexpected benefit, more often, our biases are the root of many evils.

When it comes to decision making, scientists and researchers have been driving our understanding of the processes involved in our decision making that make us vulnerable to unconscious bias. In the 1970s, it was the work of psychologists Daniel Kahneman and Amos Tversky that seems to have opened the floodgates. Tversky died in 1996, but Kahneman lived on to continue their great work.

In his writing, Kahneman often speaks of the countless hours he spent with Tversky pondering one thing or another about judgement and decision making. They were fascinated by their experiments, which involved observing others make poor judgements as a consequence of their biases.

Kahneman also observed his own vulnerability to bias. In his bestselling book *Thinking Fast and Slow*, he explains how his and Tversky's research indicates that we have two systems of thinking. Fast thinking is often automatic. When employing slow thinking, we take time to pause and think decisions through. Kahneman's fundamental premise is that we can improve our decision making by finding ways to recognise if we are thinking fast when it is a time to think slow.

> When employing slow thinking, we take time to pause and think decisions through.

Before we dig into the act of thinking slow and the role it plays in risk management, let's first consider the act of thinking fast. Because we make so many thousands of little decisions every day we would be frozen and unable to get out of bed if we did not use short cuts called heuristics; 'rules of thumb'. Say we missed a call from someone, but we assume we know what they were calling about and make a decision based on that assumption. Later we may find out our assumption was wrong. Most often, though, it will have little consequence.

Therein lies one of the issues concerning personal bias. Often it only affects us and is not particularly consequential. The problems arise when we use our shortcuts to make decisions that are highly consequential. For instance, they may concern personal safety or affect a larger number of people, such as the decisions made by organisational leaders.

> The problems arise when we use our shortcuts to make decisions that are highly consequential.

Kahneman describes more than forty mental traps we commonly fall into. Here is a small sample to give you a flavour:

- **Anchoring**. The psychological mechanism of anchoring can mean we are strongly influenced by the first thing we hear about a decision. For example, executives lock their thinking to the first estimate they hear for the budget of a project, no matter if experts increase or decrease it later.

- **Availability.** We tend to judge likelihood based on our own experience. If we know someone who has been bitten by a snake, we may tend to think snake bites are more common than others do.
- **Representative.** The representative heuristic is a bit like that old expression 'same-same' — that is, I have seen this sort of thing before, so can expect the outcome will be near enough the same. In a business context, just because a comparable product launched successfully last time and this one looks like it should follow a similar pattern, it's not safe to assume it will. There are likely several, often nuanced, differences.

Kahneman and Tversky worked hard to train themselves to identify when thinking fast was not appropriate. When heuristics were too risky and time needed to be taken to think about a situation logically, they found it difficult. Their conclusion? Simply knowing we take shortcuts when we shouldn't is not enough to improve our decision making. We need to put in place interventions.

When making decisions in your personal life, it could entail setting rules for yourself — such as, *I won't make any financial decisions in excess of $XXX without consulting my spouse/partner/accountant.*

When making decisions in organisa-

> When making decisions in organisations, we establish governance frameworks so decisions of various magnitudes are escalated to committees, the executive or the board.

tions, we establish governance frameworks so decisions of various magnitudes are escalated to committees, the executive or the board. This allows more minds to be put to work on the decision, which reduces personal bias. By default, this slows decision making down. While slowing decision making helps to overcome personal biases, if too many decisions are brought to committees and too long is taken over them, these processes form an organisational drag.

Even when an organisation has the balance right, great decisions are not guaranteed, however. In fact, according to a survey by consulting firm McKinsey & Co, executives the world over know their group decision making has plenty of room for improvement. As reported in an article by Dan Lovallo and Olivier Sibony, a 2009 survey of more than 2,200 executives showed that '…only 28 per cent said that the quality of strategic decisions in their companies was generally good, 60 per cent thought that bad decisions were about as frequent as good ones, and the remaining 12 per cent thought good decisions were altogether infrequent'.[6]

What is the cause of this underperformance? There are lots of reasons, of course, some external and some internal. One is the phenomenon of *groupthink*. According to *Psychology*

> While slowing decision making helps to overcome personal biases, if too many decisions are brought to committees and too long is taken over them, these processes form an organisational drag.

Today, the term was introduced by psychologist Irving Janis in the November 1971 issue of that journal.[7] In a 1973 paper by Janis in *Policy Studies Journal*,[8] he writes, 'I use the term "groupthink" as a quick and easy way to refer to the mode of thinking that group members engage in when they are dominated by the concurrence-seeking tendency, when their strivings for unanimity override their motivation to appraise the consequences of their actions.' He goes on, 'Members consider loyalty to the group the highest form of morality. That loyalty requires each member to avoid raising controversial issues, questioning weak arguments or calling a halt to soft-headed thinking.'

> While having committees and boards review and/or make decisions should overcome personal bias, it doesn't always overcome all the challenges of decision making.

While having committees and boards review and/or make decisions should overcome personal bias, it doesn't always overcome all the challenges of decision making. And it is not just groupthink at work. Even groups that don't exhibit groupthink tendencies are fallible because of the uncertainty surrounding bigger, harder decisions. Organisations that manage decision making best, design processes into their governance framework to tackle bias and uncertainty. Concepts may be as simple as ensuring that every business case presents three options to broaden people's thinking. And, of course, processes are needed to ensure there is appropriate assessment of risk and consideration of whether or not certain risks breach what is agreed as an acceptable level of risk taking.

A good governance framework goes a long way to helping ensure good decision making. However, there is another phenomenon besides personal bias and groupthink that decision makers need to be aware of.

Organisational bias

While groupthink is about group dynamics and the desire to conform so the group remains of like mind, there is another phenomenon at play that I call organisationthink, through which the culture of an organisation influences HOW a decision is implemented.

The effect of organisational culture on decision making was powerfully driven home for me by reading *Essence of Decision: Explaining the Cuban Missile Crisis (2nd Edition)* by Graham Allison and Philip Zelikow. You may find the book a challenge to read, but the lessons it offers are very important.

Allison and Zelikow look at decision making during the crisis through three lenses: (1) The Rational Actor, (2) Organisational Behaviour and (3) Governmental Politics. Most people are

> Leaders make decisions and staff implement them, which requires them to interpret meaning and to identify means of achieving perceived goals.

> If the need for change is not identified and managed, the initiative is likely to fail or at least be heavily impaired.

familiar with rational decision making and the effects of politics, but less so of the effect of organisational behaviour. In short, leaders make decisions and staff implement them, which requires them to interpret meaning and to identify means of achieving perceived goals. The interpretation and choice of methods of implementation are not always what the leader had in mind. There can be no better example than Khrushchev and the Soviet military machine during the Cuban missile crisis.

The Soviet mission was ostensibly a secret operation. The US was not supposed to know. But when the Soviets built missile bases in Cuba they did not camouflage them from the air. Why? Allison and Zelikow suggest it was because the Soviet forces responsible implemented as they had always implemented — according to the manual. The decision had been made not to camouflage bases in the Soviet Union to aid speed of deployment. That is, agility was chosen over secrecy. When it came to the deployment in Cuba, the message did not get through that this deployment was to be different.

The lesson for senior leaders in organisations is the importance of understanding organisational culture when making a decision in order to understand how a decision will be interpreted and whether it requires cultural change. If the need for change is not identified and managed, the initiative is likely to fail or at least be heavily impaired. A good risk assessment will always consider a range of stakeholders and how they may be impacted and/or react, given a change in circumstance.

Is the answer risk management?

This is a fair question. After all, many organisations outperformed for long periods before formal risk management programs were introduced. Yes, some failed while others thrived, and you might always suggest that all could have done better with some formal risk management. But is risk management the answer? There are many, many decision support tools available to us, as the following example illustrates.

> This is a fair question. After all, many organisations outperformed for long periods before formal risk management programs were introduced.

A few years ago, I was invited by the Company Secretary of a large listed Australian company to discuss assisting the executive and board to agree on and document the organisation's risk appetite. Here is the essence of the conversation I had as a preamble to our main discussion:

> Me: How's business?
>
> Company Secretary (CS): Great!
>
> Me: That's good! All your major projects are going well?
>
> CS: Yes, all good!

Me: How's your risk function going?

CS: Not great. People just treat it as a tick-the-box exercise.

Me: Why do you think your major projects are so successful then?

CS: Oh, we use the Red Team methodology that came out of US Defense. It's when we form a second team, the red team, and get them to critique the project team, the blue team. The aim is to check assumptions, identify potential roadblocks and look for better ways of achieving the project goals.

Me: That's risk management!

CS: Well . . . [pause] . . . yes, you're right, it is risk management.

> What is a big challenge for you may not be seen as a big challenge by someone else. One of you may be right, or you may both be wrong, but you can't both be right.

That's right. All organisations have processes in place to manage uncertainty, to guide decision making in pursuit of organisational goals. The question then becomes, are those processes good enough or do we need formal risk management?

While the Red Team methodology is a strong one, depending on how it is implemented it can have flaws. For example, identifying challenges and opportunities without having a methodology for prioritising them is the key issue. They are just a list of issues, with their relative importance open to interpretation. What is a big challenge for you may not be seen as a big challenge by someone else. One of you may be right, or you may both be wrong, but you can't both be right.

The perception of risk that each issue on the list poses, is personal. The risk process provides a way of bringing everyone's 'assessment' onto the same page. A good Red Team process will include an assessment of likelihoods, as was the case for the Red Team assessing the Blue Team's plan for assassinating Osama bin Laden. According to Micah Zenko in *Red Team: How to Succeed by Thinking Like the Enemy*, the US Department of Defense threw three Red Teams at the Blue Team's assessment of the likelihood that the person of interest in the compound was actually bin Laden. They came back with assessments of 75, 60 and 40 per cent. That was only the likelihood of it being bin Laden. No mention in his book of the likelihood of success of the mission or estimate of consequences if the mission went wrong.

The elephant in the room for the Company Secretary was not the deficiency of the Red Team approach. It is a good risk assessment methodology if it includes an assessment of risk levels. The elephant is the failure of management to ensure it

> The elephant in the room for the Company Secretary was not the deficiency of the Red Team approach. The elephant is the failure of management to ensure it gets value from its expenditure on risk.

> Is risk management the answer, when in so many organisations the risk function is ineffective?

gets value from its expenditure on risk. For this organisation, as for many others, their expenditure on risk was essentially wasted. It was to comply, not to drive success. Which leads me to ask the question again: is risk management the answer, when in so many organisations the risk function is ineffective? Look no further than the hundreds of millions of dollars spent on risk management in the financial sector in Australia that nonetheless did not avert a Royal Commission into misconduct in the industry and billions of dollars in expenditure in compensating customers, responding to the Royal Commission and associated fines.

To answer the question, let's look at some of the underlying reasons for this persistent approach to risk-as-comfort for the Audit and Risk Committee or the regulators rather than the value-adding, enabling function it's supposed to be.

3

'Risk' became a dirty word

Risk vs Risk Management

In truth, risk is not a dirty word. We need to take risks to get ahead, to achieve goals, to do great things. It is 'risk management' that is tainted! My company name when I set up my business in 2001 was Risk Management Partners Pty Ltd. I remember my mate David Morgan, who worked for Westpac (not the CEO of the same name) and who is a great marketer, came over to see me when I was first setting up. His advice: tell them what you do but make it sound bigger than it is. It was great advice. When I said my company name, people would often say, 'Oh yeah, I think I've heard of you.'

> In truth, risk is not a dirty word. We need to take risks to get ahead, to achieve goals, to do great things. It is 'risk management' that is tainted!

That company name served me well for many years. But the same things happened over and over again. At seminars or networking events, when I met someone from risk, compliance, audit or even finance, they would say, 'Risk. That's a hot space. You must be doing well.' If it was a CEO or other senior person, they would turn around and walk away as fast as they could. And that's barely an exaggeration!

> We as a profession have made risk management too complex.

CEOs and their executive teams get risk. They even use risk language. What they want is insights into the risks they are taking. What they hate is ridiculously cumbersome processes, which they often refer to as 'that compliance crap'. And that's what many of us in the risk profession have dished up to executives and boards.

There is good reason why the term risk management is tainted. We as a profession have made risk management too complex. We have nice spreadsheets called risk registers with lots and lots of columns so we can capture all the 'important bits' — Inherent Risk, Controls, Control Assessments, Consequence, Likelihood, Residual Risk, Treatments, Target Risk, Risk Owner, Treatment Owner, Action Owner — until the eyes of the poor business leader roll back in her or his head! You may have gone to any number of conferences and seminars to learn about best practice risk management. It

> Risk needs to be tailored. More importantly, it needs to deliver value.

doesn't mean that best practice is best for the organisation you serve. Risk needs to be tailored. More importantly, it needs to deliver value. If it doesn't, staff will walk in the opposite direction, or at best they will come to meetings, nod wisely, leave — and do nothing. More likely they will keep postponing the meeting. Or cancelling. Or they'll never return your call or emails in the first place!

So the main problem is how complex we make risk management for staff and decision makers. A second problem is the way we *talk* about risk.

Risk-speak

We risk people like to put risk in front of or after a word to give it a special meaning and to give us a special place in the world. Like 'appetite', 'culture' and 'reputation'. The truth is we are actually talking about something that already exists — good business practice. The best leaders consider their 'appetite' for doing certain types of business in certain ways and care very much about the organisation's 'culture' and how decisions are made, because they care about their business's 'reputation'. By putting risk in front of or behind these words we feel we create an important emphasis for leaders. Unfortunately, not all business leaders find this helpful, some seeing it merely as more red tape from the risk function.

> We risk people like to put risk in front of or after a word to give it a special meaning and to give us a special place in the world.

Worse still, when we really get going we start talking about *likelihood* and *consequence*. We start arguing over *hazard* vs *risk*. *Source of risk* vs *cause of risk*. *Frequency* vs *probability*. The *hierarchy of controls*. *Control self-assessment*. And, my personal favourite, *risk velocity*. Yes, they may be important, nuanced concepts for risk professionals, but they send 'normal' people round the bend. It's like we're speaking Parseltongue, the language of serpents in the imaginary world of Harry Potter.

And unfortunately we continue to be our own worst enemies. We head off to industry conferences, where we hear about best practice that is introducing new nuances, and we go back to our organisation with a whole new set of jargon to bedazzle leaders. To give us that special place in the world. But they're not listening, are they.

No, we need to change our language. We need to move from risk-speak to C-suite-speak when talking with the executive. To board-speak with the board. And with pretty much everyone else we just have to speak using simple, easy-to-understand business terminology. Or, better still, why not use everyday language?

Instead of conducting risk assessments,

> We continue to be our own worst enemies. We head off to industry conferences, where we hear about best practice that is introducing new nuances, and we go back to our organisation with a whole new set of jargon to bedazzle leaders.

we could be discussing challenges to successful implementation of a strategy or project. We could be discussing what must go right for this strategy to be successful. We could ask what might go wrong, and follow up with, 'And what are we doing about these things?' As a good facilitator of the conversation you will then explore whether what is being done is reliable. Is it solid?

Before your next meeting with a business leader, stop and ask yourself, 'how mature is this person's thinking about risk?' Those who have come a long way and appreciate risk management are fine with the language of risk and will use it with ease. It is the leaders in organisations with poor perceptions of the risk function who will struggle with risk-speak. The ones who see us as the 'fun police' or, another personal favourite, 'BPOs' (Business Prevention Officers). For these leaders, ask yourself how you can send the same message in their language.

> Before your next meeting with a business leader, stop and ask yourself, 'how mature is this person's thinking about risk?'

4

The agents of complexity

Complex systems

As the number one driver of uncertainty, complexity deserves more attention than most people give it. The norm is to say, 'Things are complex', and to bumble along. In this chapter I delve into the field of complex systems and introduce the notion of agents of complex systems and their effect on complexity. I then discuss some of these agents and their influence on the level of complexity you and your organisations are dealing with.

> As the number one driver of uncertainty, complexity deserves more attention than most people give it.

In her book *Complexity: A Guided Tour*, complex systems scientist Melanie Mitchell provides a layperson's definition of complexity as 'a system in which large networks of components with no central control and simple rules of operation give rise to complex collective behaviour, sophisticated information processing, and adaptation via learning or evolution'. A typical example is a school of fish. They swim along in perfectly synchronised unison, somehow knowing when to turn left or right and where to locate food and shelter. When their complex system, the school, is disrupted by a predator, the school quickly disperses, only to regroup and continue along whatever path they choose. There is no leader, just a sort of collective consciousness.

> Organisations are complex systems and each develops a form of collective consciousness that manifests in the organisation's culture.

This is important because organisations are complex systems and each develops a form of collective consciousness that manifests in the organisation's culture. To understand the importance, you need go no further than this explanation by Aaron Dignan, in an excerpt from his book *Brave New Work* on 'Changing Organisational Mindset'.[9]

Dignan explains the difference between complicated and complex by comparing it to the difference between a car and traffic. A car is complicated. It has many components. Cars with a combustion engine are powered by a chemical reaction that turns fuel into energy, which is also complicated. Yet everything about that car has been worked out by scientists and engineers. The individual components have been understood, linked together and arranged for a specific purpose: the movement of the vehicle.

Traffic also seems complicated. However, no one has yet been able to predict with certainty how traffic will flow, and hence control it. We have become better and better at understanding traffic flow and can predict what is likely to happen, but not what *will* happen. Dignan makes the point that unlike a complicated system, where we can work out cause and effect and therefore can control the system, for complex systems we can only manage them by nudging them. Dignan explains that complex systems are more about '*relationships* and *interactions* among their components than about the components themselves. And these interactions give rise to unpredictable behaviour'.

A typical example used when explaining complex systems is an ant colony. Ants of themselves are quite erratic, heading one direction then another, seemingly at random. As they encounter other ants, however, their behaviour starts to change. And as more and more ants interact, more and more 'teams' are formed to perform specific duties, such as building ant bridges to cross 'valleys', or defending the colony against attack. In other words, some form of collective consciousness emerges; hence the term used in complex systems science is *emergent*. Scientists describe an emergent system as one in which behaviours form from the relationships and interactions between elements of

> Scientists describe an emergent system as one in which behaviours form from the relationships and interactions between elements of the system.

the system. In the case of traffic, it is the interaction between vehicles.

This leads to an alternative definition of a complex system by Melanie Mitchell as 'a system that exhibits nontrivial emergent and self-organising behaviours'. Take a moment to reflect on this definition and your perceptions of an organisation. In an organisation of any size, while the leadership team thinks their strategies and decisions will be implemented in a certain way, decisions are rarely implemented exactly as anticipated. Some element of self-organising behaviours emerges, and that is the essence of organisational culture — the way we do things around here.

> In an organisation of any size, while the leadership team thinks their strategies and decisions will be implemented in a certain way, decisions are rarely implemented exactly as anticipated.

Now to Dignan's point about organisations as complex systems. He writes that 'organisational culture isn't a problem to be solved; it's an emergent phenomenon that we have to cultivate'. He goes on to explain that despite our best attempts to control an organisation through policy, process and system, it proves impossible. We end up with plenty of rules or constraints, which creates friction and organisational drag. The way to nurture the culture of an organisation, he argues, is to create the right conditions for individual decision makers to find a way to achieve organisational goals.

To illustrate the difference, and the cost of governance and compliance, let me relate a conversation I had with the CFO of a large listed Australian company. We were talking about the impact of governance and the loss of the old ways, where much more business was based on relationships. He used his sales force in an example of what happens when rules are applied. As CFO he necessarily needs to have company credit cards audited. The audit finds a few anomalies, such as entertainment expenses being incurred that were personal expenses. The lesson: 'Don't take your mate to lunch.'

So a few heads have to roll and a good chunk of money is saved as the practice halts across the sales force. Then sales go down by a lot more than the money saved. Why? Most likely because the best sales staff are risk-takers and look to work around barriers, not comply with them. It could also be that they were taking the right friends to lunch. The ones who had a connection to a connection to a good prospective client.

The attempt to control a complex system failed and more damage was caused than good. In Aaron Dignan's world, the alternate approach for the company would have been to find a way to influence the culture of the sales force to achieve a better result. He uses an example relating to travel expenses that I apply here to sales force expenses.

> The attempt to control a complex system failed and more damage was caused than good.

The company's leadership could put

it to the sales force that the organisation wants to create transparency over entertainment expense accounts and the results they drive. That is, publish the expense accounts for each member of the sales team or for each sales team — current spend, historical spend, average spend — and compare them to sales outcomes. Then allow the sales force to determine how to maximise the ratio of sales to entertainment expenses. Then, as Dignan says in his travel example, 'stand back and see what unfolds'.

This type of thinking causes a real issue for risk and for compliance practitioners that highlights a big problem. We talk so often about controls and compliance to rules and regulations, but an organisation is a complex system that, by definition, can't be controlled. If you want to test that statement, look at the Australian Defence Force (ADF). I'm assuming you would agree that the ADF is a command and control type organisation. Yet off the battlefield there has been failure after failure of the command and control model. This is evidenced in the 2015 First Principles review of the ADF, a major reform project. At the end of the report the authors cleverly created a table of all the major investigative and reform reports of the previous 15 years (of which there had been five). In the table they listed nine recurring themes relating to capability

> We talk so often about controls and compliance to rules and regulations, but an organisation is a complex system that, by definition, can't be controlled.

development of the force, then indicated in a checkbox if the same finding had been made in any of the previous five reports. All bar two boxes were checked.

There are many, many elements of an organisation that are simply complicated and not complex, and hence can be controlled. The system as a whole can't. So focus your efforts on controls and control self-assurance on complicated elements such as a production line or a payroll system. But please don't try to control the organisation as a whole. We can only nudge it in the right direction.

Now I am going to turn to agents of complexity before discussing some of the agents in play in your world.

Agents in a complex system

Where there are complex systems there is the concept of agents (another name for components). While *component* implies something inanimate, *agent* suggests an animate subject. Hence in a school of fish the components are the fish, which I am now going to refer to as agents because fish are animate.

> While *component* implies something inanimate, *agent* suggests an animate subject.

When a school of fish is attacked by a predator, the predator is an outside agent. Now consider the ocean as a complex system. The school of fish becomes an agent, and so is the predator. However, within the complex system that is an ocean, agents in the system interact. When fish find themselves overwhelmed by predators, such as a school of salmon herded by dolphins into the corner of a bay, chaos ensues and the school of fish breaks down into individual agents, which are the individual fish. After the feeding frenzy ends, the remaining agents (fish) regroup to form a school, which again becomes an agent of the broader complex system, the ocean.

Now consider an organisation such as an aged-care facility, insurance company or petrochemical company. Each is a complex system; however, they are also part of a broader complex system known as an industry. And each of these three industries has a regulator. Regulators therefore are an agent of the industry and an outside agent of the organisation. As with predators feeding on a school of fish, regulators influence the behaviour of organisations and sometimes directly the individual agents within.

> As with predators feeding on a school of fish, regulators influence the behaviour of organisations and sometimes directly the individual agents within.

Okay, okay, it's very harsh to be using an analogy of predators gorging on a school of fish to represent the impact of regulators on an organisation. Still, I think you can get my point. But let's not stop there. How about all the other outside agents, such as what I call the 'Judges', the people whose role is to look at your organisation and pass judgement, like share market investors do every day when they buy or sell the stock of a listed company?

In the next sections I explain the influence of these outside agencies and their impact on the level of complexity you need to help your organisation navigate.

Influence of regulators

I have a favourite saying about the impact of regulators when it comes to risk. Because regulators are focused on things not going wrong, and because they need to have evidence that the organisations regulated are following the regulations, regulators need documented processes and documented outcomes. So my dictum is:

> Regulators demand red tape. The risk function creates the red tape. And the business spends the rest of the time trying to avoid the red tape.

Red tape is a necessary evil. However, risk professionals need to manage it smartly. This means walking the fine line between too much and too little. Even more importantly, your job is to get the organisation into a position where it doesn't just satisfy regulators — it influences them.

> Red tape is a necessary evil. However, risk professionals need to manage it smartly.

Several of my clients are in aged care. In 2019 a Royal Commission into the sector was launched. Some, thankfully none of my clients, had massive reputation damage because their poor performance was highlighted in the hearings. Some, like Australia's largest provider, Bupa, were singled out by the media for special attention. The Australian Broadcasting Corporation analysed the accreditation reports issued by the Aged Care Quality and Safety Commission and found that 'More than half of the nursing homes ... are failing basic standards of care and 30 per cent are putting the health and safety of the elderly at "serious risk".[10]

One of my clients, on the other hand, because of their tremendous track record, sailed through almost unscathed. Yes, they had some incidents but they were few and the way they handled them was exemplary. Because of this and the work done over many years, their CEO was invited onto a government committee and was able to heavily influence the government's response to the findings of the Commission. There is hope for the aged care sector that the government's response will not be needless red tape.

Unfortunately, it is too late for the finance sector. The financial regulators around the world opted for what at the time was called the Three Lines of Defence (3LoD) risk management model. This model is simple and sounds great, in theory. The first line of defence is the business decision makers, the second line is the risk and compliance teams, and the third line is the internal

> Unfortunately, it is too late for the finance sector. The financial regulators opted for the Three Lines of Defence (3LoD) risk management model.

audit function. The inference here is that each will check the other, so the organisation has three sets of eyes looking over decision makers across the organisation.

Unfortunately, by its very nature, the 3LoD model has negative, downside risk implications: it feels very anti-agile business. So the more ambitious a management team, the more they feared it and the more they were frustrated either by it or by its implementation. To add to the problem, the language that developed around the 3LoD, language like the role of the second line is 'to provide oversight and challenge', created more trouble for risk and compliance professionals. This terminology hurts our ability to influence. The problem is that managers wish to be regularly challenged only if they are proven right, and no one, but no one, wants to be 'oversighted'.

> The problem is that managers wish to be regularly challenged only if they are proven right, and no one, but no one, wants to be 'oversighted'.

So while the 3LoD is good for the regulator as it is definitely about organisations not failing, it does not sound like it is pro-business or pro-risk taking, which of course is essential for business success. While many will argue the problem lay in how the 3LoD was implemented, the evidence is clear. Despite over a decade of implementation of the Three Lines of Defence model of risk management, globally the banks have continued to be hit with massive fines for misconduct since the 2008/09 financial crisis. In Australia the government formed the 2018/19 Royal Commission into misconduct in the finance sector. And headline-grabbing misconduct was found in spades.

Unsurprisingly the Institute of Internal Auditors reviewed the 3LoD model and in July 2020 released the Three Lines Model. The revised model dropped the word 'defence' for all those negative connotations, emphasised the creation and protection of value as per ISO 31000 and clarified roles and responsibilities of key players. I offer a critique of the Three Lines Model, in 'design' in chapter 7.

> Regulators are a strong agent of complexity. They demand red tape and they can wield a big stick.

Regulators are a strong agent of complexity. They demand red tape and they can wield a big stick. These create a level of uncertainty until an organisation has worked out how to meet the requirements of the regulator and to be best in class at doing so while minimising any adverse impact on the business.

Influence of the 'judges'

Who are the 'judges'? Earlier I gave the example of share market investors who buy and sell your stock. While they are judges of your worth, they are not the judges that cause you complexity. The judges I am talking about are the ones you interact with more or less directly. If you work for a publicly listed company, they are the analysts and the external auditors. If you work for a government agency, they are the ministers and the auditors from the Audit Office. If you are from a large, privately-owned company, it's the family-appointed advisory board. If you are from the not-for-profit (NFP) sector, it is the founders. All can be incredibly hard judges and make your world more complex.

Analysts

They are agents of complexity because there are so many of them with so many different views; and, more importantly, because their thinking is short-term. They make money for their firms if they create a reason for you and others to buy and sell stocks. A 'hold' advice won't last long because if the stock goes up or down they are wrong, and stocks are always moving. Hence you will see plenty of buy and sell positions. Analysts also need to be seen as smart, so their public commentary on your organisation, whether it is around a loss of confidence in the CEO or an opportunity to divest a business or to seek growth through acquisition, is often aimed at encouraging decision makers to act.

> Analysts are agents of complexity because there are so many of them with so many different views; and, more importantly, because their thinking is short-term.

Auditors

External auditors create complexity because you know they will come looking. Worse still, poorer auditors can have blinkers on. Like stock analysts, they have a view of how something should look in your industry or for an organisation of your size or a market segment you are operating in. This leads to a choice between following their 'conventional wisdom' and pressing on and arguing it out with them later.

Ministers

This one might be obvious to you. If you are at the whim of a minister, keep in mind that ministers change directions like the wind. Never underestimate the power of political expediency to drive their decision making. With so much uncertainty as to what the minister will be pushing next month, it is hard to plan and even harder to execute. You are forced into execution with maximum reversibility.

> If you are at the whim of a minister, keep in mind that ministers change directions like the wind.

SME Advisory boards

Like all the others, these external agents come with their own view of the world. And some appointees to advisory boards are there because the family trusts them, not because they are knowledgeable about the sector or good at being a board member. On the other hand, they may come with their own agenda.

Founders

Founders make things complicated because they are so passionate about the cause and they usually have plenty of past blood, sweat and tears in the game. They want to make an impact, and they have a view of what works and what doesn't. I have been involved with many NFPs both as an adviser and as a board or committee member (as a volunteer). I have seen it firsthand; the passion that founders have will often cloud their judgement.

> I have been involved with many NFPs both as an adviser and as a board or committee member (as a volunteer). I have seen it firsthand; the passion that founders have will often cloud their judgement.

Royal commissions

These are the mother of all outside agents. Having worked at HIH Insurance, I remember well its impact on the industry. Jail terms for the CEO, CFO and MD of Australian operations focused the minds of players in the industry. So too did the criticism of the regulator, APRA. They became focused and they grew teeth. So much so that when the GFC came along, their influence on Australian banks between 2003 and 2007/08 helped save us from the finance sector calamities we saw in the US and Europe. And when the Royal Commission into conduct in the finance sector came in 2018/19, they were let off relatively lightly compared with their sister regulator ASIC, which had not grown the same set of teeth. Having been at HIH and having clients in the spotlight in the child abuse, finance sector and aged-care Royal Commissions, I can attest firsthand to the effect they had, whether during commission hearings, when planning while awaiting the final report and recommendations, or on resourcing before, during and after the report. Emotional, stressful, remorseful, confused and uncertain are words that come to mind.

Now let's look at how we can deal with these outside agencies.

Herding the agents

> When I sit back and think about the most successful organisations I have worked with, I conjure up a leadership team that's very good at influencing outside agents, or very good at holding the outside agents to account...

When I sit back and think about the most successful organisations I have worked with, I conjure up a leadership team that's very good at influencing outside agents, or very good at holding the outside agents to account, explaining what's wrong with their requirements. Or both. They may be regulators or any of the other 'judging' agents of complexity. One example I can think of is a client in the aged-care sector. Within a short period I saw them positively influence a Royal Commission and make it very clear to authorities during the COVID-19 crisis that they would not cede control over their operations to care for the most vulnerable to the virus unless they were overwhelmed. They were highly confident they had the right systems, and that as long as they could staff their facilities, their residents were as safe as they could be. Here are some thoughts on how to herd agents of complexity from the list in the previous section.

Analysts

The problem for organisations is that they need to keep in mind the influence of analysts while at the same time influencing them on the importance of looking at the long-term vision. This is easier in Asia, where they naturally think long-term, than in the 'we want it now' western world. My observations are that the organisations that do this best get as close as allowed to analysts and always emphasise the long term.

Auditors

One of the most successful CFOs I know keeps the complexity driven by external auditors down by 'holding firm and providing credible answers'. They are smart people but they can't know an organisation in the few weeks of an audit, even if they have been the appointed auditor for a number of years.

> While some ministers will simply not care and will expect the leadership team to handle it, others will open their eyes to the longer-term implications.

Ministers

Because ministers are often driven by political expediency, their priorities change frequently. So have a list of priorities with the prioritisation criteria very clearly recorded. When the minister wants a shift, explain which of the agency's projects must be curtailed or halted in exchange. While some ministers will simply demand more and expect the leadership team to handle it, others will open their eyes to the longer-term implications. I also recommend having a good story to tell as to why you can't adapt immediately to their latest demand. Not a make-believe one. An explanation of the probable impact on people and organisations with names.

SME Advisory boards

As with any board, you need to ensure they are confident in management. Your role as a risk practitioner is to ensure that the Advisory Board, like any other board, is confident the leadership team has a good grasp of the uncertainties they are dealing with and that their strategy reflects the risk appetite of the family. If a board member comes with their own agenda, your job is to provide insights to the board that ensure this agenda, good or bad, is clearly visible.

Founders

In the NFP sector, the secret to dealing with the 'founding fathers' (to use a stale old term) is to recognise their views and design a path to influence them. It starts

> Your role as a risk practitioner is to ensure that the Advisory Board, like any other board, is confident the leadership team has a good grasp of the uncertainties they are dealing with and that their strategy reflects the risk appetite of the family.

with acknowledgement of their past achievements, their right to a seat at the table or a voice of influence. But it moves on to those the organisation serves — how their needs have changed, or how more needs to be done or done differently.

Royal commissions

Look no further than the finance sector Royal Commission. Those that played hardball lost. The highest-profile casualties were the Chair and the CEO of NAB (National Australia Bank). Working with other clients showed it was about inward reflection, honesty and responsiveness. If the commission wanted information, you did your very best to get it to them in a form they would prefer. Some industry players opted for the 'send them a thousand pages' approach. Others were much more accommodating.

> If you lack influencing skills and you poke one of these agents in the eye, you are likely to have a much more complex world on your hands.

You may have noticed how much of the response I am recommending to outside agents is about *influencing*. We all know what it is like to 'poke a bear'. If you lack influencing skills and you poke one of these agents in the eye, you are likely to have a much more complex world on your hands.

In the following chapters I unveil the true value of the risk management function, how to obtain that value and how to maintain it. I finish on the subject of influence, because being technically right as a risk practitioner has never delivered the goods. Ultimately your job is to influence leaders to be better at risk-based decision making.

5

The end game

Beyond resilience

In my early days of preaching the risk management message to boards and executive teams I would talk of the 'risk management journey'. Now some risk practitioners are well and truly over that term, though I still use it for those organisations that are on the first half of the journey.

Before I explained the risk management journey I would facilitate a discussion on the journey of a business from small to big. As a great example, I usually turn to the Microsoft Corporation. The journey started with Bill Gates and Paul Allen working in Gates' garage in Albuquerque, New Mexico.[11] Their success meant they quickly outgrew the garage, and Albuquerque, and moved their operation to Bellevue, Washington. As the years flowed by they grew and grew. Occasionally they would hit a bump in the road, such as the anti-trust action by the US Department of Justice or a product flop like Windows Vista. Mostly, though, they found new ways to grow — from MS-DOS to Windows, Xbox to Surface. No matter the challenge, they took stock of the situation, consolidated and grew some more, consolidated and grew some more ... repeat.

Once I had painted this picture, I moved on to the risk management journey (figure 5.1). I described the purpose of risk management to executives and boards as being to develop triple bottom line success by moving through four phases of growth. I would define triple bottom line success quite loosely, as it differs from industry to industry. In general, though, I would speak of $$$ and sustainability where sustainability could mean safety, the environment or a social licence to operate.

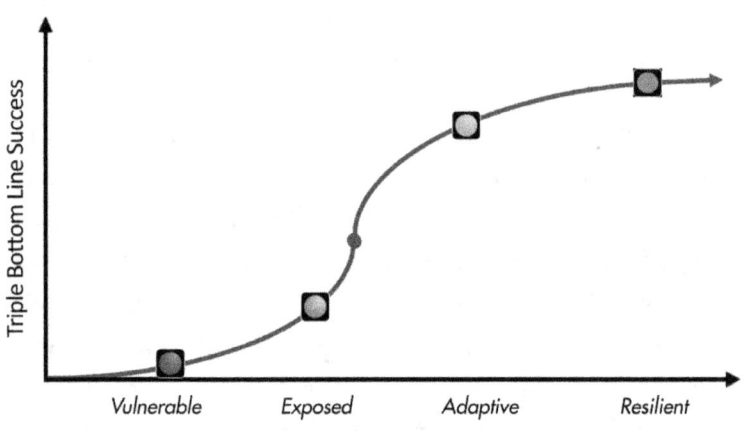

Figure 5.1: The risk management journey (four phases)

I would then describe the four phases:

- **Vulnerable** — Not even aware of the risks being taken
- **Exposed** — Some discussion about risk has taken place. Maybe they bought some risk software and ran some workshops or asked staff to think of some risks and fed them through the software. They then found they had a lot more risk than they'd known about.
- **Adaptative** — Now the organisation is managing risk, and it is using the insights gained to plan for the shifting sands ahead.
- **Resilient** — The organisation has developed a strong capacity for risk. They have a strong balance sheet or, if in government, access to funds. Their staff have developed a capability both to manage the key risks identified and to identify and manage new risks.

And there you would have it. I used to say that the end game of risk management was to become resilient. This approach served me well for quite a few years. People got it. And because they were not feeling so resilient at that stage, they would buy into the idea of becoming more resilient.

As time went by, more and more organisations 'did risk'. Either they gave someone the responsibility or they brought someone in. Some used consultants, others didn't. Either way, they moved up the curve. What I was seeing, though, was that risk management as a discipline was increasingly based on compliance. Resilience meant the regulators, the audit and risk committee and a few other interested stakeholders were feeling comfortable about the risk level in the organisation, so now they could get on and manage the business. The message to the risk fraternity was, 'Keep on doing what you're doing and keep them happy.'

> My view on risk had always been that risk management was about helping organisations to be successful.

My view on risk had always been that risk management was about helping organisations to be successful. 'Do enough to be successful — not too much, not too little', was always my advice. So when risk devolved to the role of placating others, I wasn't happy. Soon I asked myself a question: 'What makes a small business resilient?' If risk management is about seeking resilience and small businesses manage risk to survive, how do they do it without the big balance sheets? The answer, I realised, was 'agility', the ability to move faster than the giant sloth with stellar balance sheets.

Now when I present to boards and executive teams I tell them I used to stop at resilient. I ask them what makes a small business resilient, and with little or no prompting they fall upon 'agility'. Then I explain that the purpose of your risk management program should be to help you rediscover the agility that made you great in the first place. Good, fast decision making at all levels of the organisation. That's how risk adds the most value to an organisation.

I have no problem giving my audience a relevant example where agility is key to managing risk. Take the health sector, for example. For a public hospital, an aged-care provider or a pharmaceutical company, agility is essential. A public hospital must do more with less as new and often expensive technologies become available and public demand for them is created. Doing more with less is risky, so it is about achieving the same outcome faster and/or in a better way.

> Doing more with less is risky, so it is about achieving the same outcome faster and/or in a better way.

Aged and agility don't often go hand-in-hand; the industry is growing fast, however, with all kinds of stakeholder expectations and opportunities. As I mentioned before, as I write this a Royal Commission into Aged Care is taking place in Australia. Change is coming to the industry, and the ability to shift quickly will be essential for competitive advantage. Australia's largest provider of aged care, Bupa, has hit the headlines with stories of atrocious standards of care, 45 of its 72 homes failing to meet safety standards, 22 of those homes putting patients at 'serious risk' and 13 of them sanctioned, meaning they have lost government funding and are unable to take new patients.[12]

Then there are the pharmaceutical companies that must continue their quest for a portfolio of products providing sustainable cash flow, new growth and the occasional star. They must be agile in pursuing new opportunities quickly, and failing them just as fast.

The risk management journey has five phases with the fifth being agility. I use the graph in figure 5.2 to illustrate this.

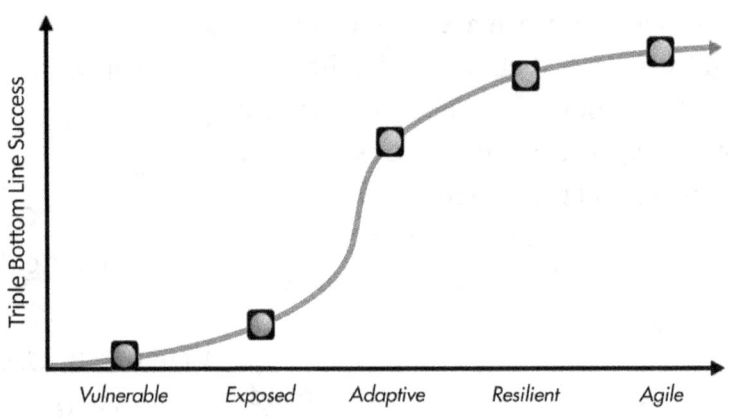

Figure 5.2: The risk management journey (five phases)

Organisational decision making

It's one thing for me to articulate the need for faster, smarter decision making and to declare that the risk management function is going to deliver it. It's another for boards and executives to fully appreciate how this can happen.

In order to answer that question, let me remind you what an organisation is. As you read earlier, Herbert A. Simon, in his book *Administrative Behaviour*, describes an organisation as a group of people who come together to fulfil a purpose. From there, management's role is to influence decision making to ensure the most appropriate decisions are made by those within the organisation to fulfil the purpose. In essence it requires that staff have the best information available for decision making so they can decide to act or not act, to hire or fire, to invest or divest, to run a project harder or abandon it. So what is the best available information, how does it get to where it's most needed and how is it moulded along the way?

I often pose this question to boards and executive teams. Before they answer I tell them about a time in 2010 when I was at a UNSW Business School seminar where David Thodey, then CEO of Telstra, was interviewed by Narelle Hooper, then Editor of *AFR BOSS* magazine, in front of about 400 people. Thodey was asked a question along these lines: 'What is the greatest challenge in running an organisation the size of Telstra?' (which then had over 45,000 employees). Thodey answered (in my words):

> *Getting information I need to know about from the extremities of the organisation to me, past all the information people are trying to tell me about that I don't need to know, in time for me to do something about it!*

I tell my audience that getting the most important information to the right people for faster, better decision making is the most important role of the risk management function. I then guide them through the following question-and-answer:

> I tell my audience that getting the most important information to the right people for faster, better decision making is the most important role of the risk management function.

'How does information we need for decision making flow through the human body to the brain?'

The brain gets information from 'the extremities of our organisation' (our body) via our five senses: hearing, sight, touch, smell and taste.

'And how is this information channelled through the body?'

Via the central nervous system.

'Where is the main information superhighway for the central nervous system?'

The spine.

'How much do we value our spines as human beings?'

A lot!

'And how much do you value the "spine" of your organisation?'

I then ask them about recent good and bad surprises that have filtered through to them from the extremities of the organisation. The organisations that are in most need of help have many. Some have fewer, but all get my point and accept they can do better. And they are interested in hearing more. After all, who doesn't want faster, better decision making by staff at all levels of the organisation? And what board or executive team would not like to reach their decisions faster and build a better track record?

To give my audience a better understanding of how they can have faster and better decision making, I look to provide them with a better understanding of how the risk management process can deliver it. By way of example, I ask them to pick one of their corporate objectives and then ask these three simple questions:

- 'What must go right to achieve this objective?'
- 'What could go wrong?'
- 'What are we already doing about these things?' (In risk-speak, these are controls.)

I suggest that many processes or activities in their organisations likely address these questions; however, none but the application of the risk management process will determine a risk level. And you and I know that risk level is important to know. While there are many reasons to calculate or estimate risk level, including the insights the process brings to the understanding of key drivers of risk, these are the three most critical reasons:

> To give my audience a better understanding of how they can have faster and better decision making, I look to provide them with a better understanding of how the risk management process can deliver it.

1. Because not everyone has the same appetite for risk!
2. To prioritise limited resources.
3. To understand the importance of some controls and whether the cost of these controls are appropriate for the risks being taken.

I will now expand on each of these. In subsequent sections I will delve deeper into the intricacies of risk management frameworks and the risk management process.

People see the world differently when it comes to risk

Before we relied on the much-used, and more recently much-maligned, risk matrix (which I will go into later), if someone in a board or executive meeting said the risk was too high and someone else disagreed, all too often the discussion would degenerate into the kind of exchange you might expect between two kids in a schoolyard.

> 'Yes it is!'
>
> 'No it's not.'
>
> 'Is!'
>
> 'Not.'
>
> 'Yes it IS!!!'
>
> 'No it's NOT!!!'

Of course, a more mature conversation would explore each person's reasoning for why they felt the risk was or wasn't too high, why one person thought that it was a reasonable risk to take and the other thought it too high.

When organisations and eventually standards organisations started documenting the risk management process, they were explicit about the need to determine what is and is not acceptable risk well in advance of a discussion about the risk of a decision, such as whether or not to proceed with a certain project.

Risk is our best-known tool for assigning resources

Whether you are the director of an opera company, a general in the army, or CEO of a large or small business, you always want to apply resources where they are most needed. In the opera company, if your chorus needs work, you will ensure they are given valuable stage time in rehearsal. If you think you can take your lead to another level to completely entrance the audience, you will ensure the right people work with them. As a general, if you feel vulnerable in certain areas, you will lend greater support to these areas. Where you think you can gain a performance advantage if you bolster a certain area, you will do so. And in business, if you think production needs to be more efficient, you will apply resources accordingly, and if you think the R&D department is close to a breakthrough, you will invest more resources with them.

> Whether you are the director of an opera company, a general in the army, or CEO of a large or small business, you always want to apply resources where they are most needed.

The difference between choosing where to apply resources, with or without an understanding of the risk levels being faced, is simply the application of a thought process. One we do pretty well naturally but that can be enhanced.

Understanding the importance of controls helps you avoid 'I could have told you that!'

How often after something goes wrong do you hear something like 'In hindsight it was an accident waiting to happen. We had so many complaints about it'? As you know, to get to a realistic assessment of risk level, you need to understand the controls you rely on for the identified risks. And you need to assess their current state of effectiveness. Not all controls are created equal, of course. Some are more effective and reliable than others. Once you understand the controls you rely on, you can decide which ones are most important by considering what might happen if they fail. Then you can answer the questions 'How important are these controls?' and 'How much certainty do I want that they will work when I need them to work?'

> How often after something goes wrong do you hear something like 'In hindsight it was an accident waiting to happen.'

And one more element. As we learned in chapter 4 from the CFO about the audit into credit card expenditure, controls need to be enough to protect and should not lead to an unnecessary burden. Even better, they should help accelerate business as leaders devolve responsibility because they know the controls are in place and are reliable.

More on these aspects of risk management in subsequent sections. Now back to faster, better decision making.

So risk management, done well, delivers a clearer understanding of the organisation's appetite for business and key priorities, and the key controls being relied on. This facilitates faster, better decision making through what I call *decision envelopes*.

> Risk management, done well, delivers a clearer understanding of the organisation's appetite for business and key priorities, and the key controls being relied on.

A decision envelope provides clear guidance to staff on the decisions that are within their realm of responsibility, how to prioritise when there are conflicting requirements to be met, and the triggers for when to seek guidance or to escalate a decision. Typically, organisations do much of this through policies, processes and systems by way of financial delegations, approved suppliers and the like. However, when risk is overlaid on these, staff have more information for managing the uncertainty surrounding them, such as when controls are compromised or jeopardised.

All this means faster decision making when uncertainties are managed effectively, and better decision making when things have gone or are about to go wrong. Good news and bad news travel faster and more clearly through the organisation. The result is a more agile organisation. That's what I offer boards and executive teams. Now, what are the practicalities of delivering on my promise?

6

Setting up for success

The thing about risk frameworks

Please see figure 1.1 (risk management through the decades) and remember there are two types of organisations when it comes to risk: those operating 'below the line', where risk management is an organisational drag on growth, and those that have risen above the line, where risk management is a key enabler of sustainable growth.

In many organisations there is a mix. Some business leaders and their teams are operating above and some below the line. If you are in the enviable position of operating above the line across the board, reading this section may help put into context what you have done well and what you have avoided. These are good to know as organisations are constantly changing, and so too must your approach. Read on and note both what you will continue to avoid and your go-to strategies. If your organisation is not above the line

> Transitioning your organisation from below to above the line requires both skill and resources. If you are near the start of the transition, your organisation sees the risk department as an impost on business.

across the board, read on for a clearer understanding of the challenge ahead.

Transitioning your organisation from below to above the line requires both skill and resources. If you are near the start of the transition, your organisation sees the risk department as an impost on business. Your job is seen as doing risk so the business can get on with business. 'Doing risk' is understood as keeping the regulators, board, and audit and risk committee happy, and trying not to interfere with the business too much. And just to make it harder, because you are not in a profit-producing area of the business, you are required to do it with precious few resources.

Don't take it too personally. You and the risk, compliance and audit professions are not alone. In a Bain & Co. article in 2013, the authors reported, 'Some 60% of business executives in our survey still believe their organisations' support functions are ineffective, cost too much or both.'[13] Furthermore, when it comes to cost savings on support functions, executives report 'only 58% successfully delivered on their targets and only 19% sustained their savings after two years'.[14] The message: senior leaders get it wrong all the time when it comes to support functions. While it is preferable for non-producing areas of the business to be as low cost as possible, under-resourcing them is courting trouble. Slowly but surely the mistakes accumulate and eventually the support function gets resourced to stop the flood.

Whether you have had your resources cut back, or you are about to introduce risk management practices into your organisation, where should you start if you are going to drive the much-needed change? The answer, as is so often the case, is to start with the end in mind.

Look at the model in figure 6.1. It shows the relationship between your risk framework and staff across your organisation. The end game for your risk framework is to drive the desired behaviours when managing uncertainty. Hence the importance of designing your framework accordingly. The model also shows that staff will have perceptions of what a risk framework is and what it is meant to achieve. And more often than not, their perceptions are misguided. They may have been exposed to poorly designed frameworks that overcomplicated things. Or they may not have been exposed to any risk framework and have perceptions of risk as being about safety and the 'nanny state', or just some more red tape to deal with. As the model shows, this means the secret to introducing and successfully embedding your risk framework relies on you providing staff with an excellent first experience of the framework, closely followed (now that you have their attention) by good

> While it is preferable for non-producing areas of the business to be as low cost as possible, under-resourcing them is courting trouble.

and ongoing engagement. In the coming sections I will provide you with a deeper understanding of the challenge and how to address it.

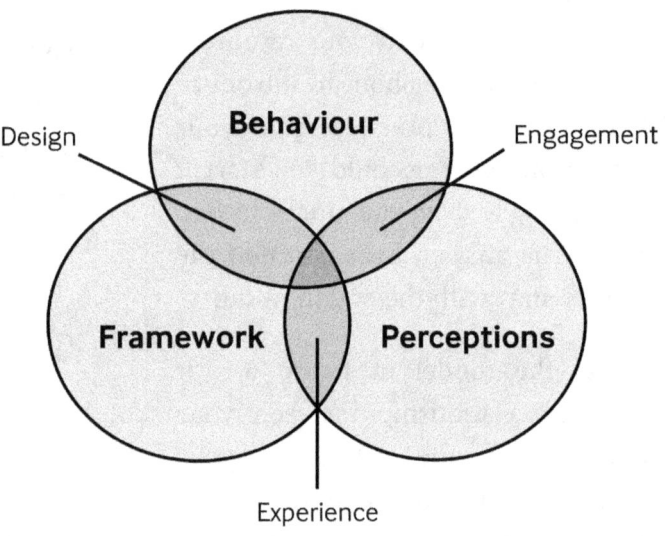

Figure 6.1: The thing about risk frameworks

Behaviours

It's all about behaviours. Culture is evidenced by behaviours, and behaviours don't lie. Which of these do you see in your organisation? And remember, these examples only scratch the surface of the wrong behaviours currently occurring across the public, private and not-for-profit sectors:

- **Senior management**: Saying risk is important while talking to their staff about everything but risk management.

- **Middle management**: Cancelling or postponing meetings about risk management. Not once — that's okay — but multiple times.
- **Frontline staff**: Ticking off checklists without thinking or, worse, without going to the work area.

At the time of writing I was in the enviable position of being designer and deliverer of the Risk Management Institute of Australasia's (RMIA) flagship risk management training program, the Enterprise Risk Management (ERM) course. Why do I consider it an enviable position? Because I was given an opportunity to help the risk profession deliver more value. To help more and more risk professionals to deliver true risk leadership in the 2020s by improving our level of influence over business leaders, so leaders of all types hold themselves and their staff accountable for managing the uncertainty in their decision making. Accountable, that is, for managing risk! If the risk profession shifts, it will be given a seat at the table where the decisions are made, not thrown the decisions after the fact and told to spruce them up to make them acceptable to audit and risk committees, or regulators or shareholders, or some other stakeholder.

In the ERM course I challenge participants to consider their role as risk professionals working within or consulting to organisations. In figure 6.2

> In the ERM course I challenge participants to consider their role as risk professionals working within or consulting to organisations.

you can see the risk themes and value proposition are as I described them earlier in the section 'Risk management through the decades'. Under the column headed influence is where I ask risk professionals to have a long, hard look at themselves. Have they read the APRA report into culture at CBA? I remind them of one of the conclusions from the report that I have already referred to:

> *'The risk function was also described as focusing on policy writing and correctness of frameworks over implementation and engagement with the business.'*

I point out that if as risk professionals they focus solely on policy writing and correctness of frameworks, they are simply an organisational drag on the business. They must focus on insights, to change perceptions and ultimately inject an urgency in their organisation's leaders, so they drive the organisation towards the desired behaviours. And that is good, considered risk-taking that recognises the organisation's capacity and appetite for risk.

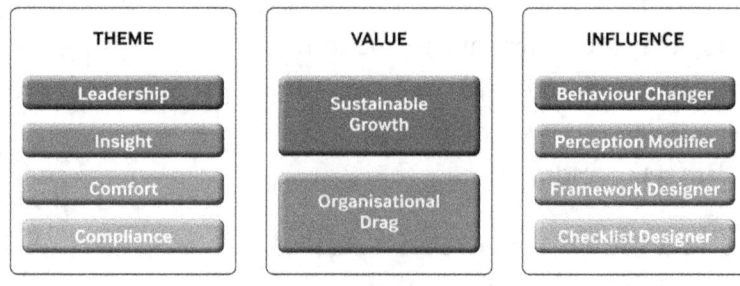

Figure 6.2: Risk leadership means behaviour change

Frameworks

Before we move on to some of the solutions available to you for driving the right behaviours, let's take a look at frameworks and their design.

Frameworks

First let's be clear on what I mean when I say framework, and therefore what it means to you. The risk management guidelines (ISO 31000:2018) state that the purpose of a risk management framework is to 'assist the organisation in integrating risk management into significant activities and functions', and that framework development 'encompasses integrating, designing, implementing, evaluating and improving risk management across the organisation'.

In my experience, different organisations use different terms to describe their framework. Some refer to their risk management plan or risk management strategy. Some use 'framework' to describe all their documents including policy, guidelines and procedures. Some consider framework as separate from policy and procedures. It doesn't matter what you call your documents, as long as it is consistent with the way your organisation works. If your organisation calls something a protocol rather than a procedure, then call it a protocol so people know where your document fits in relation to others.

> It doesn't matter what you call your documents, as long as it is consistent with the way your organisation works.

> I use policy, guideline and procedures. I prefer this approach as it keeps the detail, the procedures, out of the core guidance documents, the ones decision makers will review first.

I use policy, guideline and procedures. I prefer this approach as it keeps the detail, the procedures, out of the core guidance documents, the ones decision makers will review first. This means users are not overwhelmed with content. I find this approach works well because it provides the why, what and how of risk management in separate documents that make up the framework. Figure 6.3 illustrates the role of frameworks using a travel analogy. When travelling somewhere, we need to know the general direction in which we are heading. For me, that is the role of a policy — setting the direction the organisation is taking with respect to formalised enterprise risk management. Next we need a roadmap so we can see what we need to navigate through and around. Finally we need instructions. For example, we might decide we need to go by train, in which case we will need to consult train timetables and work out travel times, assuming time is important. If we are to travel by hire car, we may need instructions on how to operate it or on which specific roads to travel to optimise travel time or passenger comfort. These are risk management procedures or protocols.

✓	Policy	Direction	Why	✓
✓	Guideline	Roadmap	How	✓
✓	Procedures	Instructions	What	✓

Figure 6.3: The role of frameworks

This approach allows the policy to be quite brief and the guideline quite limited, maybe just a few pages. The guideline lets staff know where they can find all the detailed procedures. During the RMIA ERM course I ask participants how many pages their framework is. The answers I have received range from one page to 200 pages! The one-page reply was from a very large Australian Government agency. Their approach was to have a policy that met the intent of the *Public Governance, Performance and Accountability Act 2013* (PGPA Act), which set expectations for agencies to manage risk to help drive performance, and a framework that simply emphasised key components of risk management like decision making and culture. All the rest, even their risk appetite statement, was in procedures.

> Their approach to risk management is either prescribed or heavily influenced by a regulator of some description.

This reference to the PGPA Act highlights one of the challenges that many organisations face. Their approach to risk management is either prescribed or heavily influenced by a regulator of some description. For example, all organisations regulated by the Australian Prudential Regulation Authority (APRA) need to meet Prudential Standard CPS 220, which mandates the existence of a risk management framework, a risk appetite statement and a risk management strategy. Naturally, a regulated organisation would have documents clearly identified as these for ease of interaction with the regulator.

> The key thing you should know is that you need to design your framework to drive the right behaviours.

Let me be clear. There is no right or wrong. The key thing you should know is that you need to design your framework to drive the right behaviours. And that isn't as easy as it may sound. More on that challenge in the next section on 'Designing success', but first let's address the elephant in the room. Perceptions.

Perceptions

Whenever I am educating people about risk, whether they are board members, executives or frontline teams, I run through a little problem set on why risk management either is not working or will be challenging to implement. And the first problem I raise is perception.

So many people have a poor or incorrect perception of risk. Many years ago now I engaged a business coach. At the time my partner, Jacquie, was my business manager. We sat down for the first meeting. Without a glance towards me, he looked straight at Jacquie and said, 'So who is he?' My wonderful partner replied, 'He is one of Australia's leading risk professionals!' At that he turned to me and snapped, 'So it's your fault!'

I looked at him as I had looked at so many others. But instead of my normal response I replied, 'Don't you start. It's what I deal with every day!' Of course, I followed up with, 'By the way, what I am known for is painting risk in a very different light and changing people's attitudes towards risk management. Helping them to see that risk management done well equals value.'

If you are a risk professional reading this, you will know precisely what I mean. You will have experienced it time and time again. Being referred to as the Fun Police or a Business Prevention Officer, a wet blanket or a handbrake on business. Although we have been implementing some form of enterprise risk management in organisations for more than thirty years, so many people still don't get it. And if you doubt it has been thirty years, let me set you straight.

> Although we have been implementing formal risk management in organisations for more than thirty years, so many people still don't get it.

A close colleague of mine, Pat Barrett, is the former Auditor-General of Australia. He held that post from 1995 to 2005. While consulting to government agencies on behalf of the Department of

Finance, I had call to read many of his speeches in which he advocated the benefits of and the need for, improved risk management across government. In one speech I read, written in 1983, he referred to risk management as a cornerstone of good governance. And for the record, you can access one of Barrett's speeches from 1996 on the Australian National Audit Office website that references another speech of his from 1988 titled 'Managing Risk or Risky Management'.[15] There is your thirty years.

You may sense my frustration. But I shouldn't complain — it gives me a mission in life!

> Even if you have designed the most perfect risk framework for your organisation, their initial perception of it is almost certainly going to be negative.

When it comes to risk management frameworks, here is the issue. Even if you have designed the most perfect risk framework for your organisation, their initial perception of it is almost certainly going to be negative. When they hear about it, they will assume it is as or more complicated than the last one. If your organisation has never had one, staff who experienced risk done poorly in another organisation — and there will be plenty of them — will groan. They 'know' it's going to be painful. And staff who have never experienced a risk framework anywhere will be asking: "Why more red tape? Haven't we got enough already?"

Don't underestimate the barriers that these perceptions create. And that is why when rolling out your framework you must give your audience the most fantastic first experience of it. An experience that persuades them at least to question their perceptions, if not to cast them off. And once you have their attention you need to engage, engage, engage. Hang on to their coattails, lightly, just enough so you don't lose them, but not so tight that you become an organisational drag!

Let's now explore how you can design a successful framework revamp, introduction and rollout.

7

Designing success

Analysis

Designing success starts with designing a great framework. And I don't mean technically perfect, as technically perfect is almost certainly too heavy, overly complicated and insufficiently practical for all but the most process-minded organisations. I mean as simple and as practical as is needed to drive the behaviours you want.

> Designing success starts with designing a great framework.

In the RMIA ERM course, I run an activity where participants identify a behaviour they want to change or create in their organisation when it comes to managing risk. I then get them speed dating. They move from one fellow participant to another sharing the behaviour they want help with and receiving one idea in response. All to the sound of an appropriate music track — one I will not divulge here as it would spoil the surprise if you choose to attend the course!

After the activity is over I ask participants to share some of the behaviours they want help with and one of the good, hopefully great, ideas they received. The behaviours vary, but here are some examples:

- I want staff to stop thinking mechanically, to start thinking about risk.
- I want the board to engage with operational risk. All they are interested in is strategic risk — until something goes wrong and they are discussing operational risk!
- How to prevent managers' 'gaming risk' to receive attention or resources.
- How to prevent managers from shifting responsibility using risk — 'Now it's the Executive's problem!'
- I need to convince managers to share their risk assessments with other managers, both for transparency and to counter silo mentality.

And on it goes. Always they are very practical challenges. Unfortunately, we don't always take a practical approach to designing risk frameworks. I have seen it too many times. A risk professional heads off to a conference and comes back with 'best practice' and looks to implement it, maybe with the hope of winning an award someday, only to find that so-called best practice does not work in their organisation.

The reasons are nuanced. In a nutshell, however, either it is a poor cultural fit or the organisation is simply not primed for the introduction of risk management processes.

As explained in chapter 5, the risk management journey for organisations involves a change of state from vulnerable through exposed, adaptive, resilient and finally to agile. Each step allows a little more sophistication in the way the organisation manages risk, while maintaining 'horses for courses'. Meaning a smaller, less complex organisation will have a much simpler risk framework than a complex one such as a pharmaceutical company. Their framework would need to ensure coordination of the approach to risk across activities like R&D, clinical trials, regulator approval and patent protection. All, by their very nature, may have good risk management practices in place. However, enterprise risk management is about understanding them in the context of their potential combined effect on managing risk to the achievement of the organisation's objectives.

> The risk management journey for organisations involves a change of state from vulnerable through exposed, adaptive, resilient and finally to agile.

To any framework designer, the message is clear. You need to understand your current level of organisational maturity and identify the next level of maturity you want to achieve in the next 12 to 24 months. Identify the very specific behaviours you wish to change or create, then design your

> Every great framework design therefore starts with great analysis.

framework to create them. Every great framework design therefore starts with great analysis.

Whenever I begin working with a new organisation I start with a documentation review followed by some analysis using the tools below. It makes sense that as an external consultant I would conduct such an analysis, though it might not make as much sense to you as an internal risk adviser. Let me explain my approach, then you can decide how much value you would get from conducting a similar exercise.

Documentation review

As a minimum I look to review the organisation's website, strategic/corporate plan, annual reports, organisation chart, governance framework and, if separate, existing risk framework. I look at any existing systems for capturing risk from spreadsheets, use of risk software and incident databases. Then I dig a little deeper into operating plans and charters for board and management committees before moving on to business and risk reporting, including minutes of board and management committees, business cases, budgeting and forecasting. Lastly I ask about performance management. That includes key performance indicators (KPIs) and key risk indicators (KRIs), if they exist, and the extent to which KPIs drive decision making. That is, the extent to which managers are accountable for their KPIs.

Through the entire documentation review I am looking for evidence of how the organisation is run and, very specifically, how uncertainty is managed. What I often find is that risk is managed without anyone actually calling it risk management. The question then becomes, is the way risk is managed good enough and transparent enough, recognising that 'good enough' will vary based on the organisation? Remember the discussion I had with a Company Secretary about Red Teaming at the end of chapter 2?

> Through the entire documentation review I am looking for evidence of how the organisation is run and, very specifically, how uncertainty is managed.

Business analysis

The core analysis tools I use every time are:

- **Stakeholder analysis.** As a minimum it requires development of a list of stakeholders so the framework design does not omit anyone important, such as certain vulnerable customers!
- **PESTLE analysis.** This is a pretty standard external environment scanning tool requiring consideration of the politics, economics, social, technical, legal and environmental drivers of the business and of risk to the business.
- **Capability analysis.** This is a simple tool I designed to assess the internal capability of an organisation. The tool helps the user to consider how the organisation

is run across the five core building blocks of an organisation:

1. Strategy and Performance
2. People and Knowledge
3. Processes and Systems
4. Assets and Liability
5. Accountability and Culture

I also have a range of other tools I may use depending on the organisation and industry and their performance outlook. For understanding how their industry operates I often use Porter's Five Forces, which helps me to understand their business model. I may also use value chain analysis for organisations with large or complex supply chains, and I will use a Unique Selling Proposition (USP) tool to get an understanding of their competitive advantage and what is at stake.

You can find all of these tools, along with examples, in the learning resources section of my website bryanwhitefield.com.au/learningresources. Better still, you can learn in detail how to use some of these tools if you take the RMIA ERM course.

Behaviour analysis

Once I have conducted my research I start to discuss the behaviours sought. For example, has the organisation had a number of financial mishaps recently or has it sustained significant regulatory breaches? Or, at the other end of the spectrum, are they doing very nicely for all the right reasons, and simply seeking a slow and steady uplift in management of risk, for example through the use of more data and/or data analytics in decision making.

Whatever the case, the behaviours sought are noted. Next comes design.

Design

What ultimately determines the design of your framework is the risk management model that will best suit the organisation and its culture. When it comes to the type of risk management model you could implement in your organisation, there are two extremes. On the one hand, you could keep the risk function very small and put all the emphasis on the business to manage its own risk. On the other, you could create a much larger risk function where people with risk-related roles recognised in their title are operating within business units. The former describes what many people call the Risk Champions model; the latter is more like the Three Lines Model I referred to in the 'Influence of regulators' in chapter 4.

> What ultimately determines the design of your framework is the risk management model that will best suit the organisation and its culture.

In the RMIA ERM course, I run an activity in which I split the group into two and ask one side to convince the other they should have a risk champions model and the other to argue for the Three Lines Model. Invariably both models will have their fans and by the end of the activity most participants will agree that some hybrid model of these approaches would work best for most organisations. Some remain wedded to the risk champions model because of the attitude of management that the back office should remain lean and the front office accountable for their decisions. Some remain wedded to the Three Lines Model because it is all they have known, or is more or less required by the regulator, or is preferred by their professional body (usually the Institute of Internal Auditors) and consequently preferred by the Audit and Risk Committee. Some will feel strongly that the business simply can't yet be trusted, so the Three Lines Model makes sense for them.

> While I have been a strong critic of the Three Lines Model because of the harm it has done in creating perceptions of risk as a compliance function, I am actually a hybrid devotee.

While I have been a strong critic of the precursor to the Three Lines Model, the Three Lines of Defence model, because of the harm it has done in creating perceptions of risk as a compliance function, I am actually a hybrid devotee. I prefer what I call a Tripartite Model of Risk Management. Before I go on to explain it, rest assured that both a risk champions model and a Three Lines Model can work, in theory, but understand that they are hard to accomplish. And when they are accomplished you are most likely looking at a tripartite model — a model built on accountability, mutual respect and trust. And accountability, mutual respect and trust are established only at the highest levels of maturity of governance of an organisation.

Next I explain the tripartite model and then move on to helping you introduce it with a great first experience and to build ongoing engagement. If your organisation is not yet mature enough for this approach, I outline in chapter 11 how you can work towards it from your organisation's current level of maturity.

The Tripartite Model of Risk Management

It is inherently difficult to make fantastic decisions all the time without allowing our personal biases — not to mention time pressures, performance pressures and the fact that sh!t happens — to affect our judgement. In order to counteract our failings as decision makers, we introduce processes within a governance framework. Larger, more significant decisions are taken out of the hands of line managers and escalated to higher authorities, whether it be individuals, committees, executive teams or the board. However, even highly experienced executive teams don't get every decision right. And as you and I know, risk management is designed to help.

> It is inherently difficult to make fantastic decisions all the time without allowing our personal biases — not to mention time pressures, performance pressures and the fact that sh!t happens — to affect our judgement.

A mature organisation recognises these challenges and is keen for a risk function that delivers true insight and value. If that is what your organisation wants and is ready for, then here is the path to better decision making.

Form a tight partnership between business, risk and internal audit with the intent of managing the complexities of the business together, not as one layer checking on another, and not using part-time risk advisers with a bigger day job to fulfil, but as a truly integrated tripartite partnering relationship.

> The risk function is responsible for providing business decision makers with insight into decisions and providing the internal audit function with insight into the key controls on which the organisation relies.

Figure 7.1 shows the key elements of tripartite risk management. The business is responsible for decisions. The risk function is responsible for providing business decision makers with insight into decisions and providing the internal audit function with insight into the key controls on which the organisation relies. The internal audit function is responsible for ongoing assessment of both the quality of decisions and the reliability of the controls to provide assurance to the most senior leaders that it is all working, that the business is making decisions within their risk appetite and that the risk function is providing good support through the insights delivered.

Below I look at each function in more depth.

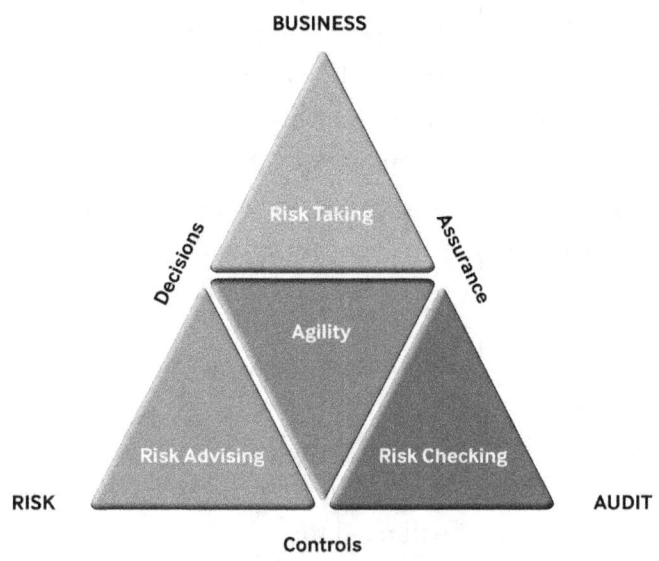

Figure 7.1: Tripartite Model of Risk Management

Business

The role of business is risk-taking. You need to take risks to create value. As I have noted, however, you need to take risks with 'eyes wide open', meaning you are aware of the risk you are taking, and why, and are as comfortable or uncomfortable as you want to be. Or

> The role of business is risk-taking. You need to take risks to create value.

you have the permission of stakeholders to take risks you would not normally take because you have little choice. Sometimes the largest drivers of risk are outside our control and we just need to push on regardless.

> In the tripartite model, the business is accountable for the decisions made. There's no risk committee to get approval from.

In the tripartite model, the business is accountable for the decisions made. There's no risk committee to get approval from. While the business may have a steering committee that performs a similar role, it is not a risk committee saying yes or no. It is business leaders gaining an appreciation of the risk involved and making a call.

In your framework you need to clearly articulate their responsibility for assessing and managing uncertainty in their decision making. That means they will need to:

- Agree on their appetite for taking risks to achieve business objectives (risk appetite).
- Establish guidelines for ensuring risk is considered in key decisions and that the guidelines are within the organisation's appetite for risk or are escalated accordingly, typically in business and project planning, in governance committees and in response to significant events, such as issues escalated to the executive or board for decision.
- Ensure their policies, processes and systems guide staff business-as-usual (BAU) decision making so decisions are within the organisation's appetite for risk or escalated appropriately.

- Review and allocate resources to provide assurance within business units that controls can be relied on.
- Share risk information across the business where appropriate and in a timely manner to facilitate risk-based decision making.
- Ensure performance and risk reporting are inextricably linked and reported on simultaneously.

You can find a simplified example of integrated performance and risk reporting in the learning resources section of my website bryanwhitefield.com.au/learningresources. You will see that each objective has a risk rating. I explain how the risk levels are derived in 'The start of good risk assessment' in chapter 10.

I cover integrated performance and risk reporting in more depth in the RMIA ERM course.

Risk

The role of the risk function is to help the business and internal auditors with risk thinking. The risk management process is the best tool known to humankind for managing uncertainty. As experts in the process, risk professionals' role is to help others to develop and adopt risk-based thinking.

In the tripartite model, the risk team is

> The role of the risk function is to help the business and internal auditors with risk thinking. The risk management process is the best tool known to humankind for managing uncertainty.

small relative to the size of the whole organisation and is all about decision support. There is no outsourcing of risk-related work from the business. If it needs more resources, then the business hires the resources required and ensures they understand and apply the risk process that is appropriate for their role.

The small risk team is there to provide advice through regular conversations with business leaders about the decisions they are making and the processes they are employing to manage the complexity that makes their decisions uncertain. The team facilitates workshops on request, not because the risk framework demands it. The reason they are requested is because they provide insights. They add value.

> Through the design of the risk framework, the risk team provides benchmark standards for business leaders to meet and/or aspire to.

Through the design of the risk framework, the risk team provides benchmark standards for business leaders to meet and/or aspire to. Standards for managing risk in BAU decision making, in programs and projects, and in business planning and execution. There will also be standards of transparency — what is visible to whom and when, whether through formal reporting or not. And those standards will be blue ribbon, not red tape for the comfort of someone else. They will be created through a business outcomes lens, not a traditional risk lens.

In summary, your framework will need to clearly articulate the risk function's responsibility for:

- Analysing and providing insights to the business to assist them to identify and understand risk.
- Providing benchmark standards for the business to work towards, including reporting and sharing risk information.
- Providing the tools, templates and techniques that will allow the business to understand risk.
- Communicating to the audit function the controls the business is most dependent on.
- Working with the business to rectify deficiencies identified in audits and to share better practice across the business.
- Ensuring the business has access to adequate specialist resources to manage risk, whether that be specialists in cyber fraud or simply good workshop facilitators or quantitative risk modellers.

Audit

The role of internal audit is to check and assure. Independently. This means audit should be separate from the risk

> The role of internal audit is to check and assure. Independently. This means audit should be separate from the risk function as they need to check both the decisions made by the business and the advice of the risk function.

function as they need to check both the decisions made by the business and the advice of the risk function. Audit should be left alone to assure independently while being encouraged to provide their advice in the clearest and most positive form, so the business and the risk function are most likely to heed their advice.

In the tripartite model it is the audit team that will check, on behalf of business leaders, if risk-taking by the business was within the defined appetite for risk set by the board. The audit team will also check if the risk benchmark standards are being achieved.

> Your risk framework will need to clearly articulate the responsibilities of the internal audit function.

The audit team will also assess if the benchmark standards set by the risk team are meeting the goals of the organisation, if they observe any deficiencies in the quality of advice given, or in how the advice was communicated to the business.

Your risk framework will need to clearly articulate the responsibilities of the internal audit function, including:

- Demonstrating its ongoing independence of both the business and the risk function.
- Confirming the reliability of key controls via long-term audit planning.
- Conducting performance audits of frameworks, programs, projects and processes, including an assess-

ment of how the business is managing risk within its appetite for risk.
- Periodic assessment of the performance of the risk function to engage, inform and influence the business.

There you have it. My version of organisational nirvana. I appreciate that achieving it will be tough. To help you along the path to righteousness, I have included a sample risk management framework using the tripartite model for a small organisation in the *learning resources* section of my website, bryanwhitefield.com.au/learningresources. Irrespective of the size of your organisation it should give you a good feel for the approach and how you might design your framework.

Now, how are you going to introduce your new framework to the world?

Experience

Remember what I said about perceptions? Everyone has their own, and you can guarantee some will be negative. When you introduce your new framework, people won't necessarily be expecting anything good. So your job is to give them a great experience, which will open the door to ongoing engagement.

> When you introduce your new framework, people won't necessarily be expecting anything good. So your job is to give them a great experience, which will open the door to ongoing engagement.

Let's start with a few *don'ts* and some corresponding *dos*:

- Don't put the framework up on the internet with a policy signed by the CEO. Do sit down with each area of the business individually to work through the why, how and what of the framework.
- Don't start with middle management or below. Do start with the executive team. If they are truly behind it, the rest will happen over time.
- Don't rely on management and staff's assumptions and interpretations of the framework being correct. Do create a simple means of communication for staff to query and clarify the why, how and what for them.
- Don't start with risk reporting. Do start with risk insights to teams, beginning with the executive.

> The most common thing I hear after a workshop for executives who have not had a good experience of risk is this from the CEO: 'Thank you. That's not what I was expecting. We have never had a conversation like that before.'

This last *do* is my go-to method for ensuring a great experience for the most important group — the executive. You hear it so often in risk: you need 'tone from the top'. I know you might be over that phrase, so choose another one. But the idea is key. And running a risk workshop for the executive is key to winning them over. Sometimes I call it a risk workshop, sometimes a strategy implementation workshop, sometimes simply an insights workshop, depending on the culture and maturity of the organisation.

Another course I run for the RMIA and for organisations with lots of risk staff is Mastering Risk Workshop Facilitation. I tell participants that the most common thing I hear after a workshop for executives who have not had a good experience of risk is this from the CEO: 'Thank you. That's not what I was expecting. We have never had a conversation like that before.'

I tell course participants, 'When you hear those words or something similar after a workshop for people who don't really appreciate the value of risk management, you know you've nailed it.' This should be your aim.

> 'When you hear those words or something similar after a workshop for people who don't really appreciate the value of risk management, you know you've nailed it.'

How else might you give staff a great first experience of the new risk framework? There are plenty of ways. Here are a few:

- Arrange for senior management to introduce the framework to each of their key direct reports.
- Ensure senior management have a meaningful conversation about risk when their team provide their first risk assessment.
- Double down on your efforts on researching the business challenges a team has before your first

engagement with them to ensure you provide at least one impressive insight. How might you be sure you are doing so? Ask their boss or someone else you feel comfortable with who would be a sound judge.

- Acknowledge that something they are already doing is excellent risk management without being called risk management (using the Red Team methodology on projects, for example), then demonstrate how it can be enhanced for their benefit.
- Use a case study in which applying the risk management process found massive opportunity for the organisation. My favourite was my experience with an equipment leasing company which discovered through risk assessment that they were losing 20 per cent of their gross profit on pretty much every major client because of a misalignment between sales and service.

The gist of this is to get inventive. Stand in their shoes. How are you going to surprise them? Pleasantly!

Now you have their attention, don't let go. Engage, engage, engage until the behaviours change. The next section will give you some ideas how.

> Like so many things in life, you can't have it all NOW. Patience is key.

Engagement

Like so many things in life, you can't have it all NOW. Patience is key. And working smart is the way to go.

Just as the risk champions vs Three Lines Model can be operated at both ends of the spectrum, so can engagement. At one end you have money and resources, and you can run a full-blown change program as if you were introducing a new Enterprise Resource Planning (ERP) system. If you have won over the executive so they are wanting change, and fast, you presumably will be given a fair amount of money and resources. So get to it. You don't need much help from me. Identify a successful change program in the last year or two, go speak to the authors and leaders of that program, and basically copy it.

> Identify a successful change program in the last year or two, go speak to the authors and leaders of that program, and basically copy it.

If you are not in that enviable position, here are some thoughts on what you can do.

Communicate your why

You may well have heard of Simon Sinek and his golden circle, introduced in his book *Start with Why*. In it he argues that people don't 'buy' from you for what you do; they buy from you for why you do it. So the *what* of risk management needs to wait. You first need to communicate your *why*.

In the RMIA ERM course, I break the group up into a number of teams and ask them to prepare an 'elevator pitch' to a senior executive explaining what the risk function does. Some do better than others in the little time I give them, but

> Charities in the not-for-profit sector will often see success as fulfilment of their charitable mission while associations see it as member satisfaction.

across the groups they all get the gist. It needs to be short, sexy and not boring, and must talk about helping others to be successful in whatever terms they perceive success. For example, some for-profit organisations will see success in terms of growth rate, others in terms of market share. Charities in the not-for-profit sector will often see success as fulfilment of their charitable mission while associations see it as member satisfaction. And in government it can be anything from accuracy of budget forecasts to doing more with less to pleasing the minister. You need to work it out.

Next, put it on your email signature block and start a newsletter with it featuring as a tag line.

Communicate the what

Why start a newsletter? Because newsletters can work. Just ask bestselling American author Seth Godin. In his aptly named book *Tribes*, he tells a fantastic personal story about what can be done when you build a tribe. In 1984, at the age of 24, he joined a tiny software company called Spinnaker and was charged with acquiring science fiction stories and turning them into adventure games. He was given no staff and had no programmers directly assigned to him. He was lent three programmers from the pool of 40 working on other key projects. He needed many more programmers to meet his Christmas deadlines.

He started a twice-weekly newsletter about his little tribe's quest, telling the story of what they were working on and what they were achieving. Seth made photocopies for each of the one hundred plus staff and dropped it into their in-trays (yes, millennials and post-millennials, 1984 was a time without email!). Within a month, six more programmers were working with his group whenever they had spare time. 'Then it was twenty. Soon every person in the entire department was either assigned to my project or moonlighting on it.' They made their deadline with five products and every one of them went 'Gold'.

Pretty simple really. Tell them what you and others are working on to help drive the success of the organisation, then tell them about what is being achieved.

> Tell them what you and others are working on to help drive the success of the organisation, then tell them about what is being achieved.

Now you may have noticed I have left out the 'how'. The how is of course contained in your risk management framework, but I would not recommend going around touting the framework. Instead, focus on encouraging good practices that are fulfilling the intent of the framework wherever you see them. Especially if they are not called risk management but, for example, problem-solving workshops or cross-functional meetings to break down silos.

Build your team of advocates

As I mentioned, the most common conclusion drawn from the activity of comparing a risk champions model with the Three Lines Model is that a hybrid is the best way to go. That is, even if in the Three Lines Model you include risk professionals in frontline business, you should also have risk champions. People from the business unit know this implicitly, have authority and are influential. They don't need to be risk experts. In fact, it's better if they are not.

In the next section I go into some detail on how to go about developing your risk champions so they become your tribe of advocates. A tribe of advocates will help maintain positive engagement with the risk function even when no one from risk is in the room.

Advocates

Building a tribe of risk champions is all about building a tribe of advocates. Before I go into describing how you build a tribe, refer to figure 7.2. It compares how you are perceived by the business units you serve and the quality of the relationship you have with them. If you are operating below the line, you are fighting recalcitrants

> If you are operating below the line, you are fighting recalcitrants rather than building lasting business partnerships that are both mutually respectful and highly productive in helping to drive the organisation towards its goals.

rather than building lasting business partnerships that are both mutually respectful and highly productive in helping to drive the organisation towards its goals.

Below I work through the different levels of the diagram so you can think about your relationship with your various internal clients in more depth.

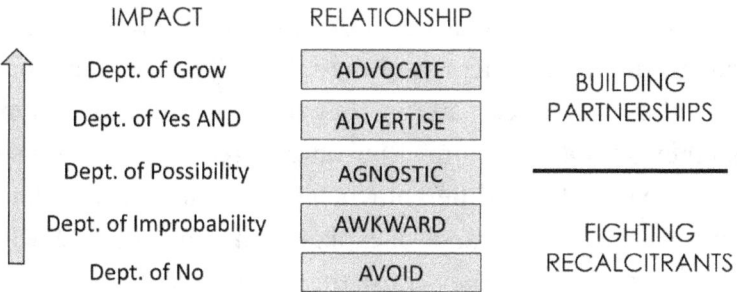

Figure 7.2: The Relationship Ladder

They avoid you

The bottom of the ladder is obviously the worst place to be. Those you and your team need to engage with avoid you. Sometimes it's subtle. Perhaps they keep postponing meetings until it's too late, leaving you with little room to manoeuvre to help them in the way you feel would be best for the organisation.

These stakeholders most likely see you as the Department of No, whose sole purpose is to put a handbrake on their progress. They feel the policies, processes and systems you have put into place are red tape and that they can't run their business if they comply in anything more than the smallest way.

Hopefully you don't have too many of this type!

They are awkward around you

When the relationship is awkward your client is most likely 'playing the game'. They know they have to deal with you; they know you have a job to do that means some level of engagement with them, and they don't like it. If they don't play the game at least a little, they might get told to comply, so they do the minimum. They often agree with your advice then do something different when it suits them. They offer a range of explanations when you ask why they chose the different path.

> Clients often agree with your advice then do something different when it suits them.

These clients are still definitely recalcitrant and, while they don't see you as outright blockers, they feel it is highly improbable that you are going to add value to their business beyond what they already know and do.

They are agnostic towards you

It is almost as annoying if they are agnostic towards you. They will do what is needed. They know how it works. They want to get it done with the least amount of angst. They don't see the value, but they are practical types. They know the organisation would not be spending as much as it does on you and your team if the executive didn't believe it was necessary. Most will even entertain the possibility that what you do helps them on occasion get better results. After all, they don't see themselves as perfect.

They advertise you

Now we move into much more comfortable territory. These stakeholders get what you do and why you do it. They engage and work with you and the results show. They are good advertisements for you and your team. Many of them will even acknowledge the good work you have done for them and will say so to their management.

> These stakeholders get what you do and why you do it. They engage and work with you and the results show.

The reason they advertise you is because they understand that you are not saying 'no', you are saying 'yes and', meaning they feel you are working flexibly with them to find solutions to help them get the results they need in a sustainable way.

They advocate for you

I hope you have a few of these stakeholders. They are great to work with. They get what you do and have their own insights into how you can help them. They push you to higher standards than you even thought possible. They set you challenges and seek out your creativity. They relish the prospect of you bringing your solutions to their problems so they can build on them. They achieve outstanding results.

They don't just acknowledge your great work with their

management hierarchy; they actively promote you to other departments. They even question why other departments are not working with you as they do.

They see you not as the Department of No!, but as the Department of Grow!. The department that provides them with not just a good reliable service but valuable insights, challenging them to work to higher standards than they thought were possible.

Take a few moments, grab a piece of paper or open an electronic note, and map your stakeholders to each of the levels on the Relationship Ladder. A good question to ask yourself as you do this is why they are where they are? As you find answers to these questions you will find things you should do more of, and maybe some you should do less of.

Now let's look at risk champion tribe building.

Building a tribe

The first step in building your tribe is selection. Your preference should be for working with the leaders you wish to partner with and guiding their selection of staff you are going to nurture. Obviously, there is a bit of a trick to how you will couch this. Using the terms *risk champions* or *tribe* is not necessarily the best approach at first. A safer option

> Your preference should be for working with the leaders you wish to partner with and guiding their selection of staff you are going to nurture.

might be to express the need to develop a *community of practice*.

When you design your tribe, don't think 'sphere of influence'; it actually needs to be more pear-shaped — that is, focused at the top on leadership and broader at the base, and juicy. If you already have risk specialists in the business you have been working with for some time, they need to be in your tribe to work across the broad base and to deliver the juice. However, you also need carefully selected, business-savvy influencers. Being savvy, they will be able to understand the intent of the risk framework so they can identify how best it should be embedded in their business unit. Being strong influencers, they will be able to deliver the message effectively.

> If you already have risk specialists in the business you have been working with for some time, they need to be in your tribe to work across the broad base and to deliver the juice.

Once you have identified your tribe members, your objectives should be to nurture collaboration amongst the team, challenging them and helping them develop creative solutions to drive the outcomes you are seeking (see figure 7.3).

Collaborate

You need this team to be collaborating as a team. The more they collaborate, the more they will gel, despite not being

> People like a challenge, and a team of people who have gelled like a challenge even more. Work with them to identify the problems they can help you solve.

co-located. The more they gel, the more their collective wisdom and efforts will play out.

Challenge

People like a challenge, and a team of people who have gelled like a challenge even more. Work with them to identify the problems they can help you solve. A really, really common one is that risk is overlooked or forgotten prior to the big decision being made. Once the decision is made, someone up the chain who is somewhat concerned about the decision will then ask risk to review it. Sometimes you end up identifying plenty of problems with the decision, in the nicest possible way, yet they feel you are being negative or out to create a roadblock. So identify this problem with them and see what the collective genius comes up with to ensure risk is considered early.

Create

This is where the rubber hits the road. You need results. You need them to co-create with you how the risk framework will be implemented in their business units.

Building a team that is collaborating, challenged and creating great stuff can be highly rewarding. Here are a few tips on what to focus on as you build the team.

The Three Es

When building your tribe, always remember the three Es. In order to ensure strong collaboration, you need to focus on how best to Engage them. When you set challenges, focus on what is most likely to Excite them. And above all, make sure the tribe Enjoy themselves. Create the right environment and facilitate with the three Es in mind, and you are most likely to end up with a high-performing team.

If you think about it, what you need to do is what your favourite teacher used to do. The classes you remember most will be the ones when you needed to collaborate with classmates to tackle the challenges set. It was the greatest opportunity to be creative. You were engaged, excited at the prospect of taking on the challenge, and you enjoyed the process of creating your solution.

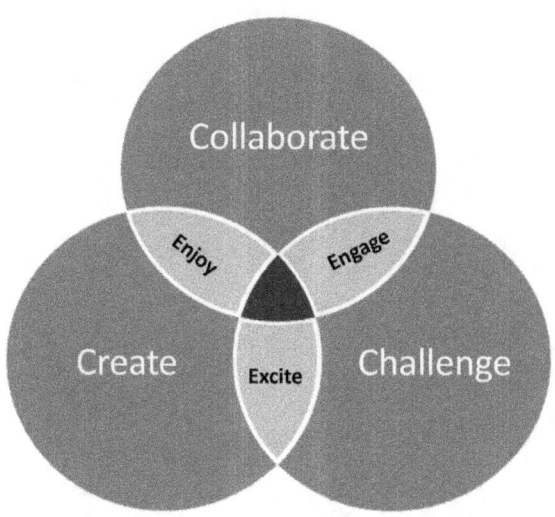

Figure 7.3: The three Es of tribe building

Having got this far you now have all you need to develop a high-level risk framework that will meet the needs of the business. In the next few chapters I discuss some of the more challenging aspects of a risk framework — appetite, KRIs and getting maximum value from risk assessment.

8

Appetite for business

Does it matter?

A great deal of information about risk appetite statements is available to risk professionals. Some has been generated by regulators, who publish better practice guidelines or prescribe specific requirements for risk appetite statements; more is produced by industry associations and service firms. Maybe you have had some success with these sources, maybe not. I have helped many organisations with them, so let me give you my thoughts on them and whether they really matter.

First and foremost, we all have an appetite for risk. No one wraps themselves up in cotton wool and hides away from the world to live life absolutely risk-free. Second, appetite for different types of

> No one wraps themselves up in cotton wool and hides away from the world to live life absolutely risk-free.

risk varies from person to person. Some of us will not risk our health by smoking cigarettes but will jump at the chance to sky dive; others smoke but would never dare to sky dive. Third, every day we take our individual appetite for risk to work and apply it to our decision making. Staff need to understand the organisation's appetite for risk-taking and that it overrides their personal beliefs. Lastly, a risk appetite statement should be firmly embedded in your organisation's strategy. It's all about understanding the opportunities ahead and the potential risks in pursuing them, and about making clear decisions on which ones to pursue and how aggressively. Thankfully, the need to link risk appetite and strategy is clearly articulated in the most recent COSO (Committee of Sponsoring Organizations of the Treadway Commission) guidance on risk appetite.[16]

> A risk appetite statement should be firmly embedded in your organisation's strategy.

To be honest, when I first heard about the drive for documented risk appetite statements, I thought it was being dreamed up by consultants to make money. What I came to realise was that I understood the risk appetite of an executive team because I was facilitating risk workshops for them. It was all the staff not in the room with us that were having a problem understanding it.

While a regulator's requirement or a desire for best practice have been drivers of some organisations whose risk appetites I have helped document, the main reason people have come to me is the best reason: because middle management is unclear on the board's or the executive's appetite for risk *in fulfilment of the organisation's strategy*, and the board and/or executive want help articulating it as succinctly and effectively as possible.

However, your board or executive team may simply be ticking a box with risk appetite. If that is the case, start with this. Highlight for them the problem of individuals applying their own appetite for risk and ask them this question: 'Are many people in the organisation spending time on things that are unimportant to you and not spending time on aspects of the business that are important to you?'

> 'Are many people in the organisation spending time on things that are unimportant to you and not spending time on aspects of the business that are important to you?'

The answer to this question is likely always to be yes. The bigger question is, to what degree? The greater the gap between their expectations and reality, the greater the benefit they would derive from driving an understanding of risk appetite deep into your organisation's DNA, resulting in staff spending more time on value-creating activities, and less on activities that are less important, or not important at all!

There's one more phenomenon you need to understand, however. It became very clear to me years ago when I was running risk champions training for a team tasked with putting workers in a high-risk and emotionally stressful environment. I was talking about the need to design policies, processes and systems to guide decision making 'so staff will make the same decision the CEO would make'. Then, from the middle of the pack of 25 in the room came, 'Bullshit! The CEO would not know shit when it comes to some of the decisions we need to make.'

> Leaders hire staff with specialist skills to get the job done.

Of course he was right. Leaders hire staff with specialist skills to get the job done. The CEO can't be a specialist in all areas. So what happens in organisations is that senior management are trying to influence decision making below them and out to the extremities of the organisation. Meanwhile those at the extremities are looking back at the executives in their 'ivory tower' and saying to themselves, 'They have no idea!', and they try to influence the executive. And poor middle management is caught in the middle.

It's like what happens when two magnets are brought close to each other when the poles are reversed (figure 8.1). The flow of the magnetic field from north to south is interrupted. Getting risk appetite right is the beginning of alignment of the poles, where decisions are made within appetite, or are escalated if they are not, and information is fed back to decision makers to increase the knowledge and overall capability of staff throughout the organisation.

I believe risk appetite matters. BUT it is not as easy as saying, 'Let's have one.' I'll explain more about the challenge then provide you with some insight into how you can help your organisation develop or improve its risk appetite statement.

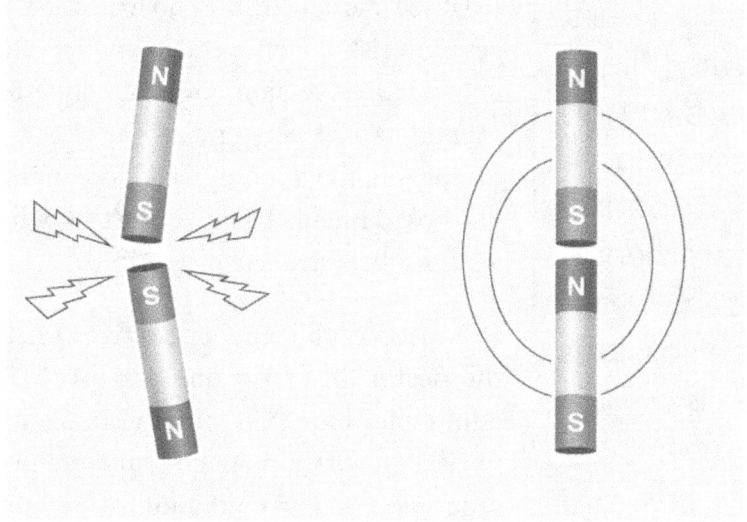

Figure 8.1: Risk appetite — aligning the poles

What makes it difficult?

Before I go into why it's difficult to document a risk appetite statement, let me say this: helping organisations with risk appetite is the single hardest thing I do. Full stop! It is hard to articulate, harder and often emotional to achieve agreement. Let me give you an example from when I assisted the board of a health district here in Australia.

Your typical health district runs hospitals as well as a range of community services to promote health and manage issues such as mental illness within the community. The boards are made up of clinicians, administrators and community representatives.

I battled hard with this board to get a genuine risk appetite statement agreed. It took three sessions over a couple of months. At the very end, as the ink was drying on the final agreed document, one board member said, 'I don't see why we can't just have one paragraph!'

> I battled hard with this board to get a genuine risk appetite statement agreed. It took three sessions over a couple of months.

Let me put this in perspective. First, the desire to go for one paragraph is admirable; indeed, I preach simplicity in risk. However, managing uncertainty requires a certain amount of rigour. Second, the board member probably felt comfortable having one paragraph because he had been in the room for all the discussions we had around risk-taking. A few small examples:

- The first position was that all of the strategic objectives, from acute care through mental health services through population health, were 'essential'. When I asked which ones would be discontinued if a pandemic hit the area and 30 per cent of staff were off sick while demand for services had gone off the charts, they soon realised their appetites for achieving certain goals were quite different.

- Patient safety with regard to the behaviours of some clinicians. Doctors work long hours. Some ignore guidelines on managing fatigue and press on regardless. Was this acceptable or not? Things to consider were whether the fatigue guidelines were appropriate and the potential backlash from doctors if they were held to account for breaching fatigue guidelines.
- Keeping the lights on. Recently there had been several power outages that disrupted one of the main hospitals. A report had been prepared that recommended a relatively large investment in backup power, money that could be spent on mental health or combating smoking and drug abuse. What was the board's appetite for risk of a disruption of several days to a hospital vs more funding for key services?

These issues need discussion and appetite for risk agreed. The hard part is then articulating it so decision makers can understand it well enough to apply it in similar and not so similar circumstances. That is why I always draw up the model for boards and executive teams shown in figure 8.2. The model helps discern the quality of a risk appetite statement. I ask the board and/or executive which type of statement they want. One that is fluffy and false and

> The hard part is then articulating it so decision makers can understand it well enough to apply it in similar and not so similar circumstances.

damages the culture, or one that is convenient, uninspiring and will change nothing. *Or* one that is genuine, enduring and will help strengthen the culture of the organisation.

Of course the reply is always genuine and enduring. Then they fight tooth and nail to avoid words and statements that are anything more than uninspiring rhetoric, such as:

- We have a very low appetite for safety risk.
- We have a high appetite for innovation using technology but a low appetite for cyber risk and for disruptions to technology services.

My question to them at this point is, who doesn't?

Yes, it is difficult to articulate risk appetite. I have seen 'more blood spilt on the boardroom floor' from discussions on risk appetite than on any other topic. So don't go into this thinking it will be easy or without collateral damage. I believe it is worth the risk, though.

The next sections will make your job a little easier, though it won't be risk-free either for you or for others involved.

> Yes, it is difficult to articulate risk appetite. I have seen 'more blood spilt on the boardroom floor' from discussions on risk appetite than on any other topic.

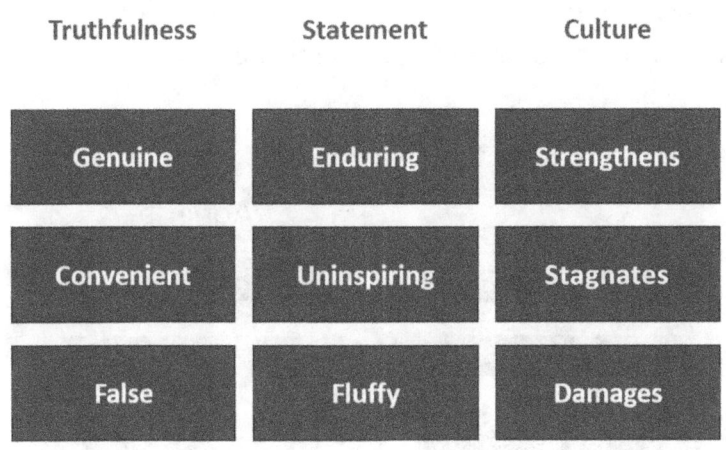

Figure 8.2: Quality of risk appetite statements

Risk appetite framework

I know, I know, another framework. Yes, I see risk appetite as needing its own framework so the main enterprise risk management framework is smaller and less daunting for staff. Yes, the risk appetite framework is positioned within the risk management framework so staff know it exists and where to find it, but it is not a focus for all staff. Just senior decision makers. The reason for this is that I believe risk appetite is set by the board, championed by senior management, operationalised by middle management and lived by staff (see figure 8.3). In practice, staff need to be guided to make decisions within risk appetite through policies, processes and systems. And middle management need enough understanding of appetite so that they can implement the needed policies, processes and systems to drive the organisation towards strategic goals. This is what I refer to as operationalising risk appetite.

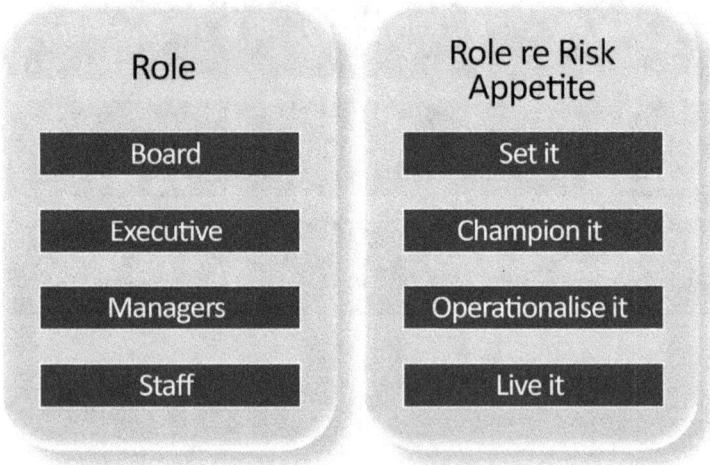

Figure 8.3: Risk appetite by role

Before I explain how to develop a risk appetite statement, let's examine the three components of a risk appetite framework: capacity, appetite and tolerance (see figure 8.4).

Capacity

This term relates to your organisation's ability to take on risk. With any risk decision you have to think about your ability to manage the business to achieve the core objective, to manage the uncertainty around it and to bear the consequences if the risk event does eventuate.

Appetite

A formal definition in the international standards is the 'amount and type of risk that an organisation is willing to pursue or retain' — in other words, what we are willing to risk to achieve the goals we have set. For example, are you willing to partake of a local custom of 'facilitation payments' to government officials to win government contracts? This might give rise to a moral or values-based type of appetite for risk. Or, are you willing to lose $7 billion in pursuit of a new treatment for breast cancer? You may choose to take such a financial risk because of the potential upside and your confidence in the research team developing the treatment.

> A formal definition in the international standards is the 'amount and type of risk that an organisation is willing to pursue or retain' — in other words, what we are willing to risk to achieve the goals we have set.

The challenge with appetite is always expressing what is an intricate subject comprehensively but succinctly when developing a risk appetite statement that is genuine and enduring, and that strengthens your organisation's culture.

Tolerance

This is about the setting of boundaries. The process of establishing the minimum and the maximum risk to be taken in pursuit of your objectives. The line in the sand you must cross and the line in the sand you will not cross. For example, 'We must invest $3 billion over the next three years to find a new treatment for breast cancer. However, we will not exceed a total commitment of $5 billion over the same period.'

Tolerances are relatively easy to determine when it comes to financial risk. It gets harder when talking about people's lives or customer service.

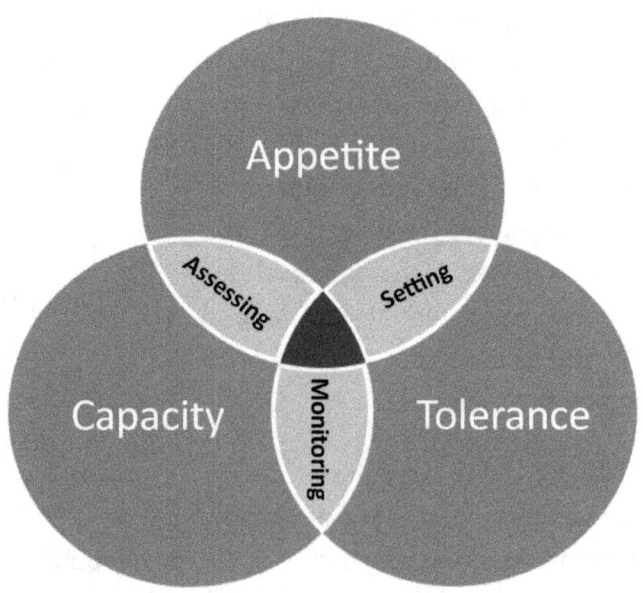

Figure 8.4: Risk appetite framework

Developing risk appetite statements

Refer again to figure 8.4, which shows the relationship between each of the three key components of the risk appetite framework: assessing, setting and monitoring. The organisation's appetite for risk taking can only be set based on an assessment of the organisation's ability to take on risk. Once you have set your appetite, you need to monitor the organisation to confirm whether you are operating within the agreed appetite for risk taking.

Assessing capacity

To assess your organisation's capacity to take risks, you need to consider the ability to manage risk and the ability to withstand the impact of events should they arise. Being good at managing risk does not mean bad things will never happen.

> When I help leaders of an organisation assess organisational capacity to manage risk, I conduct a risk maturity healthcheck.

When I help leaders of an organisation assess organisational capacity to manage risk, I conduct a risk maturity healthcheck. The assessment looks at five key building blocks that make up an organisation:

1. Strategy & Performance
2. People & Knowledge
3. Processes & Systems
4. Assets & Liabilities
5. Capability & Culture

This risk management maturity model is different from most as it is not an assessment of your progress in implementing technically correct risk management guidelines, using language like *basic* or *repeatable* or *optimised*. It is an assessment of how agile your organisation is in making risk-based decisions. The five maturity levels I use come from the S-curve I introduced in chapter 5 (figure 5.2), where Agile is the most mature level. I have found this methodology to be very helpful for senior leaders as they will much more readily assimilate words like *vulnerable*, *adaptive* and *agile* than basic, repeatable or optimised.

The rating system takes each element and breaks it down into the five sub-elements shown in figure 8.5 As you can see, these are standard elements of an organisation. The maturity assessment is not an assessment of whether an organisation has a risk process that has resulted in the development of risk registers or other typical artefacts of risk management frameworks. It is an assessment of whether the organisation has put in place suitable processes for managing uncertainty in pursuit of organisational objectives. This might sound complicated but it's important. Let me explain.

Remember my discussion with the Company Secretary of a large corporate about how they managed projects successfully, recounted in chapter 5? The answer given was Red Teaming, bringing in a review team on a major project to see how well the project was planned or was progressing. When assessing an organisation's project risk management, I would rate them favourably if they were doing Red Teaming very well, particularly if they were rating risks identified in the process using the organisation's approved risk criteria. Risk management can be achieved in many different ways, but fundamentally it is about quality over 'correct' application of guidance documents like ISO 31000.

Another piece of the risk appetite puzzle that deserves to be highlighted is the ability to bear the consequences of risk. In my risk maturity healthcheck I address this through the sub-elements of asset and liabilities. These sub-elements highlight for senior leaders how vulnerable or resilient their organisation is to the impact of risks occurring. A strong balance sheet is obviously key, but so are the other sub-elements that protect the balance sheet. That might be anything from insurance and management of potential legal liabilities, through strong contract negotiation and documentation and

> The ability to manage uncertainty should be a key consideration when determining strategy and setting targets.

ensuring key assets (tangible or intangible) are managed effectively over the long term, to allowing for timely renewal of fixed assets and financial planning as intangible assets lose their legal protection or competitors catch up.

A solid assessment, such as my risk maturity healthcheck, drives the critical conversations you need to have with your board and executive team *before* risk appetite is set, and, in an ideal world, *before* the organisation's strategy is set. After all, the ability to manage uncertainty should be a key consideration when determining strategy and setting targets.

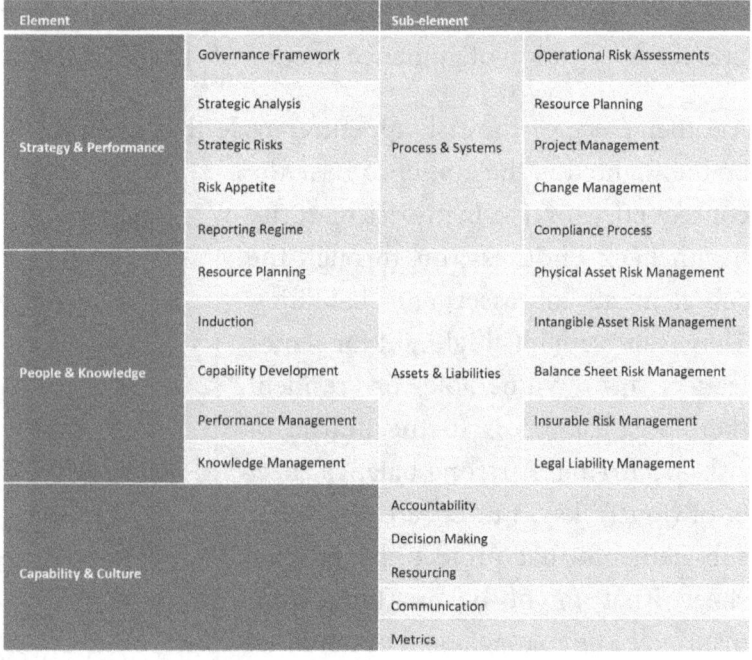

Figure 8.5: Risk maturity healthcheck rating elements

Setting appetite

There is no right or wrong answer to how you set appetite. I will say, however, that I think documenting risk appetite by risk category only is incomplete. Every risk appetite statement should be linked to strategy. I have developed and trialled several methods over the years. They boil down to three key types of statements:

1. **A general statement.** A statement reinforcing the values of the organisation and highlighting the risks that need to be taken and those the organisation tries to minimise. The statement typically is about one page in length and covers the key areas of safety, finance and regulatory compliance. It also highlights the types of activities, such as in research and development, that must be undertaken if the organisation's purpose is to be fulfilled.

    I usually recommend this approach if the organisation's risk maturity is low. Recognising that they are all difficult to reach agreement on, this is the least difficult and so produces less friction between board and executive, within the board and among the executive.

2. **An objectives-based statement.** One written statement for each strategic objective describing the minimum and maximum amount of risk to be pursued in working towards achieving the objective. Often this approach will include examples of the types of activities there is a strong appetite to

pursue and others that are to be avoided if possible. This approach is also often accompanied by visual indicators of risk appetite, such as traffic lights.

I recommend this approach for mature organisations that want a robust discussion and deeper clarification of the risks to be taken and those to be avoided. It requires strong facilitation skills to minimise friction and to ensure all involved buy into the end product. A strong advantage of this approach is that it provides greater guidance to management, which makes it easier to discover what can be measured and to identify if the organisation is operating within the defined appetite.

3. **A swim lanes approach.** In this approach, four levels of risk appetite are described, such as *controlled, cautious, accepting* and *open*. These become swim lanes. Appetite for risk-taking is set by placing each strategic initiative, along with key programs and frameworks, into one of the swim lanes. For example, a strategic initiative to open an operation in a new country might sit in any of the lanes depending on the size of the investment and the view on how capable the organisation is to deliver. For

> Appetite for risk-taking is set by placing each strategic initiative, along with key programs and frameworks, into one of the swim lanes

something like regulatory compliance in a heavily regulated industry, the compliance program may sit in the most risk-averse lane, *controlled*. Similarly, for a government entity the procurement framework might sit in the *cautious* lane while for an innovative private-sector company it might sit in the *accepting* or *open* lane.

> Once appetite is set using descriptors, it is common practice to establish a set of risk tolerances that are often called key risk indicators (KRIs).

The advantage of this approach is that it is highly visual and requires much less careful use of appetite descriptors. It works best for organisations that have well-defined strategic initiatives, programs, projects and frameworks. It also promotes an understanding that some new initiatives may naturally have to have an open or accepting risk appetite. As the maturity of the initiative increases, its upside and downside will become clearer and may become more controlled.

You can find examples of each of these types of statements in the learning resources section of my website bryanwhitefield.com.au/learningresources.

Monitoring performance

Once appetite is set using descriptors, it is common practice to establish a set of risk tolerances that are often called key risk indicators (KRIs). As with every aspect of risk, it seems to be easier to focus on the downside; however, understanding risk appetite is as important for ensuring your organisation seizes the right opportunities — that is, takes sufficient risk to be successful in the long run. The late 'systems thinker' Dr Russell Ackoff once wrote, 'The deterioration and failure of organizations are almost always due to something they did not do.' KRIs should be set with lower and upper limits.

For example, an organisation may decide that there should be a healthy level of ongoing innovation. In this case, you could set a lower and upper financial limit of investment in innovation projects. If the level of investment is tracking below the lower threshold, questions might be asked. It may be that there is too much red tape for new projects or that funding has been pulled for one reason or another. Either way, management can investigate and decide if action is required or if it is acceptable to operate outside appetite for a while.

> If the organisation consistently operates outside of the agreed tolerances, then the capacity they thought they had must not be there.

This leads to a point I like to make to boards and executive teams. Tolerances are there to measure whether or not they were right when they assessed the organisation's capacity to manage and bear risk. If the organisation consistently operates outside of the agreed tolerances, then the capacity they thought they had must not be there.

They will either have to shift appetite or do something to build capacity.

Being an engineer, I am a measurement kind-a guy. I'm not afraid of numbers and I love the challenge of quantifying difficult things. If you do too, I highly recommend *How to Measure Anything* by Douglas Hubbard. In his words, if you can observe it you can measure it. Whether you pursue measurement comes down to the cost of acquisition of the ability to measure vs the value it will deliver.

> Whether you pursue measurement comes down to the cost of acquisition of the ability to measure vs the value it will deliver.

Herein lies the trap when it comes to KRIs. Sometimes there is a tendency to overcomplicate things by measuring too many indicators, because there are so many indicators you can measure. Take financial indicators, for example. There are sales stats, cost of goods sold stats, liquidity ratios . . . and on it goes. Most may already be measured, and for good reason. They may be used to fine-tune performance of the sales team or the supply chain, or to demonstrate financial stability to creditors. When it comes to developing KRIs, I suggest measuring the bare minimum. Let the business fine-tune and only worry about the big-ticket items.

When it comes to sales, for example, can you do some modelling to find out the biggest indicator of future sales? Is it the unemployment rate, the weather or the number of hits on your e-commerce website? If it is a good enough indicator, just monitor that. Sometimes it won't be just one thing. For example, cost of goods sold might vary based on oil price, weather and lead time for order fulfilment. In such a case, measure all three but report it as one KRI. That is, the COGS (cost of goods sold) KRI.

There is no need to get bogged down in the detail. Leave that to the fine-tuning of performance in the business. The role of risk tolerances is to let the business run its game and only raise a warning if necessary. By the way, if the business does not do fine-tuning using metrics well, don't try to fix it using risk appetite. Help them see the benefit of data and indicators to fine-tune their business. You are a risk partner, not a surrogate manager of their business.

> Help them see the benefit of data and indicators to fine-tune their business. You are a risk partner, not a surrogate manager of their business.

And don't fall into this trap. One client I worked with followed the objectives-based statement method. For each statement we were able to identify one or two KRIs, for which we set lower and upper boundaries. The problem was that some of the KRIs were measured only annually or bi-annually. So when it came to reporting time, either there was nothing relevant to report, because the data was out of date, or a whole heap of work went into trying to measure it.

One last item on the topic of tolerances. Can you measure

culture? The answer is yes. Culture is observable. Therefore, as per Hubbard, it is measurable. The question for you is, is it worth measuring any more carefully than how overall culture is traditionally measured — via a culture survey? In some organisations, such as those regulated by APRA and those who experienced a Royal Commission into misconduct, it is. Misreading your culture and having major issues that draw the attention of the regulator or, worse, the media, could be career limiting for many involved.

> The question for you is, is it worth measuring any more carefully than how overall culture is traditionally measured — via a culture survey?

Operationalising risk appetite

I mentioned earlier that risk appetite is set by the board, championed by senior management, operationalised by middle management and lived by staff. In practice, this means staff need to be guided to make decisions within risk appetite through policies, processes and systems. And middle management need enough understanding of appetite so they can implement the needed policies, processes and systems to drive the organisation towards its strategic

> The method I use for operationalising risk appetite, in order to use it to influence decision making, I call decision mapping.

> Once a decision map is prepared, policies, processes or systems can be prioritised for development or improvement as required.

goals, which is what I refer to as operationalising risk appetite.

The method I use for operationalising risk appetite, in order to use it to influence decision making, I call decision mapping. It means the development of a decision map that documents the policies, processes and systems in place and their ability to guide decision making within appetite for risk. Once a decision map is prepared, policies, processes or systems can be prioritised for development or improvement as required. An example of a decision map is shown below in figure 8.6. The map starts at the highest level, the organisation's strategic goal or mission statement, and works down to strategic priorities and the appetite statement for each priority. From there the *translation points* for the appetite statement are the key organisational policies and frameworks, such as the performance framework, procurement, finance and HR. Each one is then assessed as to whether or not it clearly guides staff to operate within appetite for risk. The classic examples are financial delegations and procurement frameworks — who is able to sign off on what and within what limits.

Once you have identified policies, processes and systems that need improvement, the rest comes down to how urgently you need these improvements and the resources available.

If your organisation is performing reasonably well, I would urge you not to rush it. It will be better in the long run if you design changes that are as simple but effective as possible.

In the next chapter I discuss the challenges of monitoring your organisation to see that it is within risk appetite and some practical tools for further linking risk appetite to strategy.

> Once you have identified policies, processes and systems that need improvement, the rest comes down to how urgently you need these improvements and the resources available.

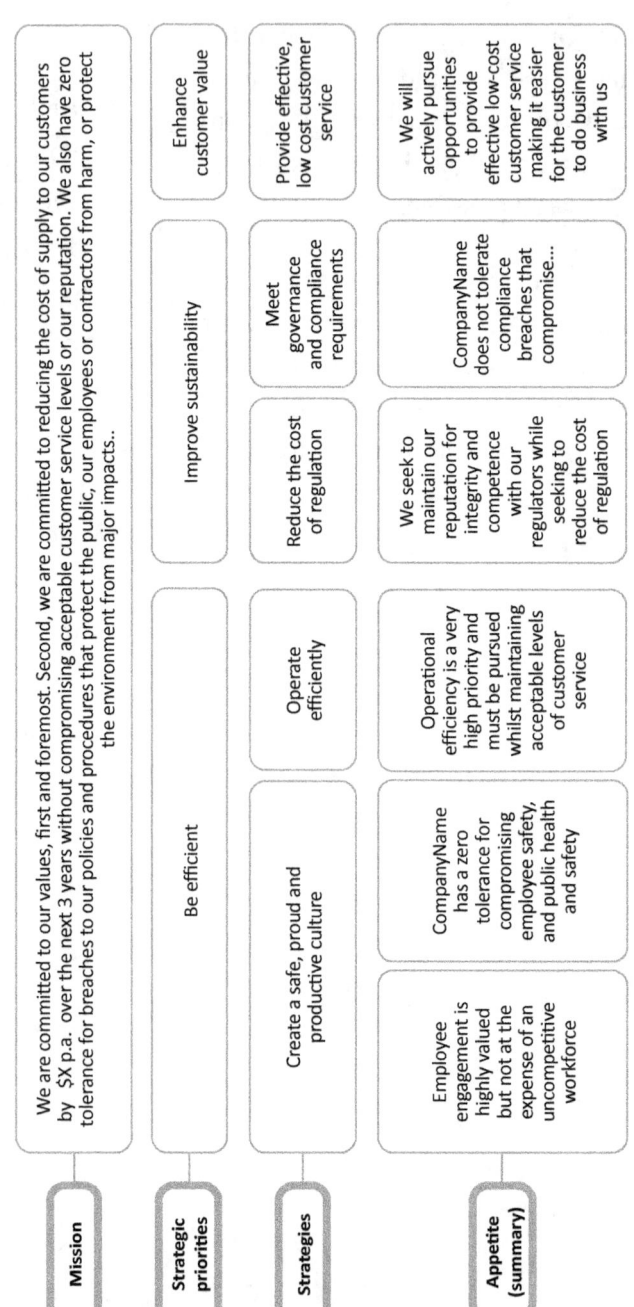

8: APPETITE FOR BUSINESS | 151

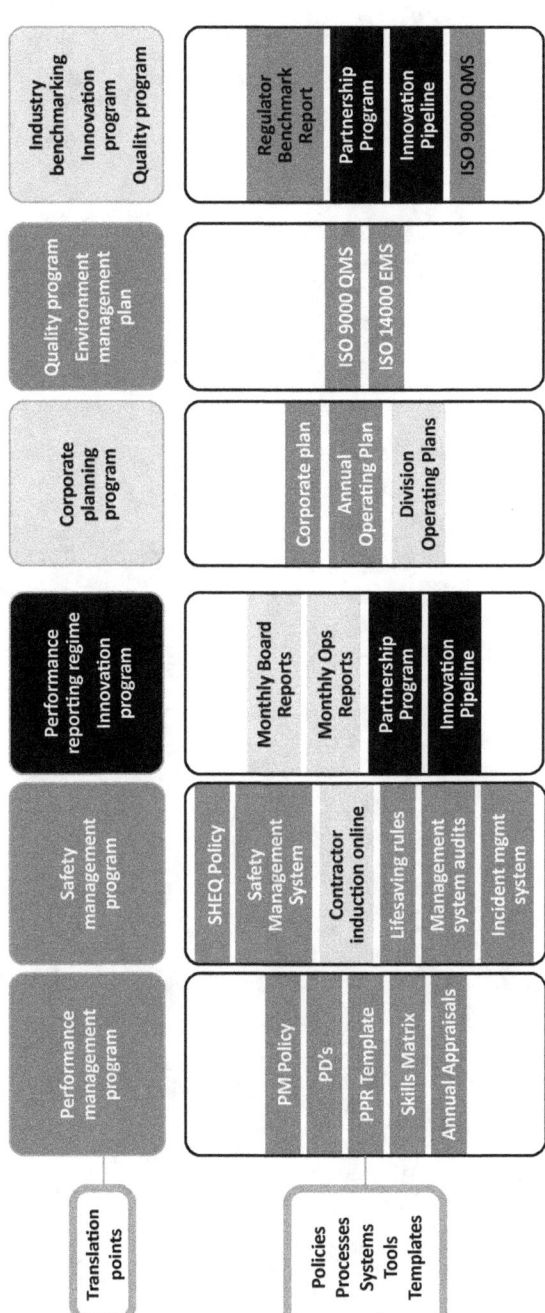

Figure 8.6: Sample decision map

9

Reading the Signals

Signals are the secret to sustainability

Author's note: I wrote this chapter before COVID-19 hit. I'm sure we are all now extremely familiar with the potential impact of major disruptions to our work and personal lives. And all wish that governments globally had read the signals from SARS and MERS, and that coronavirus vaccine research had not been put on hold. Hindsight is wonderful. As you read this chapter, remember the next set of disrupters are waiting patiently. Some are not waiting at all.

We can't predict the future with accuracy,

> All wish that governments globally had read the signals from SARS and MERS, and that coronavirus vaccine research had not been put on hold.

> Those organisations that survive and thrive through the stunning growth in complexity we will see over the next decade will surely be masters of navigating complexity.

this I am sure of. Those organisations that survive and thrive through the stunning growth in complexity we will see over the next decade will surely be masters of navigating complexity. I use the word navigating advisedly, because if you are unaware of how your organisation's world is shifting in these complex times, you won't be able to manage your way through as effectively as you might. Signals are the secret to sustainability.

Think about the advent of personal computers in the 1980s, email and the internet through the 1990s and the globalisation that followed in the 2000s. In that decade Facebook, Twitter, Instagram and the first smartphone were all launched. Airbnb and Uber also started their disruptive charge. This past decade we have seen the rise and rise of streaming, big data and robots running on AI and machine learning generating new ideas most of us have trouble getting our heads around. Think blockchain and cryptocurrencies, drones delivering parcels, the League of Legends video game that runs 'World Cup' events and the instant phenomenon that was Pokémon Go.

Think about the pace of change created in your life by these events. Now multiply it by a factor of ten as the changes of the last decade become mainstream and new ones arrive.

Driverless cars, to be followed by flying cars; 3D printers creating a house; miniature drones following you on the golf course so you can watch your game from a bird's-eye view when you get home. Can't wait!

What is the risk if you don't read the signals well? The impact is obvious: restructures, buy-outs, insolvency. What of the likelihood? While history is no guarantee of the future, a quick Google search will tell you the average lifespan of companies is falling. At one end of the spectrum, there are some companies that are over 1,000 years old.[17] At the other end, the failure rate for public US companies within five years has increased from 1 in 20 to 1 in 3 over the past 50 years.[18] While there can be a multitude of factors at play, from a growth in entrepreneurial attitudes to oil shocks and global financial crises, one has to recognise the basic shift to high-technology companies (Google, Apple and Microsoft) and an associated transformation of industries through the creation of new business models enabled by technology (Airbnb, Uber).

> While history is no guarantee of the future, a quick Google search will tell you the average lifespan of companies is falling.

The pace of change is snowballing. How much is it increasing? I love the out-of-this-world thinking of Tim Urban and the crew at waitbutwhy.com, and feel the graph in Urban's blog *The AI Revolution: The Road to Superintelligence* captures what is in front of us perfectly (figure 9.1).[19] It's kind of funny and scary at the same time. And it is the scary bit that I believe should galvanise you to get very good at reading the signals for your organisation or, better still, work with the business to read the signals. Let's start with performance indicators.

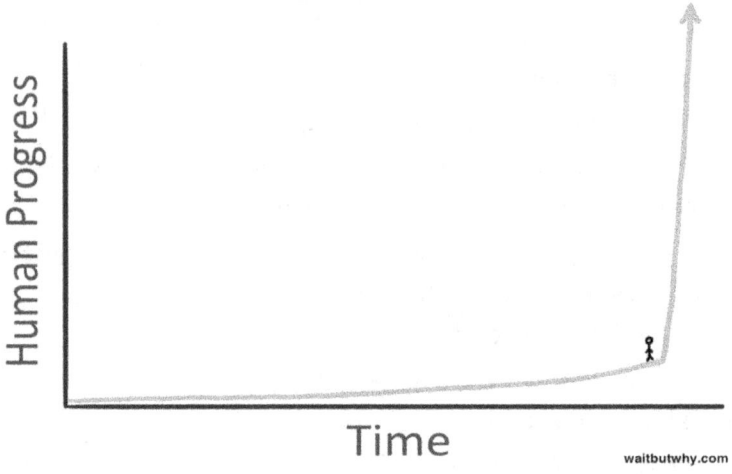

Figure 9.1: Human progress vs time, by Tim Urban, waitbutwhy.com

KPIs and KRIs

Key performance indicators (KPIs) have been part of the business lexicon for a long time. In 1956 V.F. Ridgway published a paper titled 'Dysfunctional Consequences of Performance Measurements' that starts with the sentence 'There is today a strong tendency to state numerically as many as possible of the variables with which management must deal.' So we can safely say KPIs have been a 'thing' for at least 70 years. What of key risk indicators (KRIs)?

First let's be clear. A KRI is simply a subset of a KPI that is commonly referred to as a lead KPI. KPIs are either lead or lag measures: lead, for where we are heading; lag, for where we have been. An example of a lag indicator is profit. An example of a lead indicator of profit is the number of new customer enquiries received via your website. In this example, if you established a high correlation between the number of new customer enquiries and the number of quotes and acceptances by customers, and they were highly correlated to the level of sales, you could suggest the number of new customer enquiries as a KRI, for the risk of not meeting profitability targets.

Given that a KRI is simply a lead KPI, when I work with organisations to develop KRIs I start by asking them, how good are your KPIs? Eighty per cent admit they are poor. If KPIs are done poorly, it makes it very difficult to do KRIs well. If you don't know what measures matter, how can you know what signals to read? At least they are not alone. The problem has been around for decades. In his 1956 paper, V.F. Ridgway wrote, 'What gets measured gets managed — even when it's pointless to measure and manage it, and even if it harms the purpose of the organisation to do so.'[20]

> Given that a KRI is simply a lead KPI, when I work with organisations to develop KRIs I start by asking them, how good are your KPIs? Eighty per cent admit they are poor.

Now that we have established the importance of good KPIs

and KRIs and the lack of success many organisations have had in developing them, let's look into how to develop measures that matter.

Measures that matter

KPIs are a decision guide for your staff. They are a guide to what constitutes good customer service, what is a good profit margin, what is a good return on assets employed. And they should be a guide to what truly matters to your organisation. Unfortunately, because we are so damned busy when we finish identifying our strategies for success, we do what so many have done before us and pluck KPIs from wherever we can find them. We reuse the old, we google to see what others are using and we sit around a table kicking a few ideas around, and presto, here are the KPIs.

Unless you are lucky and your organisation came up with very good KPIs, you are likely to see one of these things happen. They are simply ignored and everyone keeps doing what they have always been doing and only watching the headline numbers. Or the KPIs tend to be biased, even for those organisations running the balanced scorecard concept. And as we found out during the Royal Commission into the Australian finance sector held over

> As we found out during the Royal Commission into the Australian finance sector held over 2018, the bias was against customers, especially the least aware and the most vulnerable.

2018, the bias was against customers, especially the least aware and the most vulnerable. In fact, we were provided with a smorgasbord of examples of KPIs driving the wrong behaviour despite good intentions of identifying what really mattered — sales and consequently profit. There could have been no better example than that of the tellers at CBA putting a little of their own money into kids' bank accounts to meet targets set for new kids' bank accounts, thus earning themselves bonuses!

The best KPIs inform and guide people to consider a range of factors contributing to a decision. The same is true for KRIs. But first you need to know what measures really matter, and that starts with KPIs. If your organisation does not have good KPIs, then that is your first job as a risk adviser. Point out the risk and see that they are improved. I frequently help organisations improve their KPIs. However, if you want a thorough and deliberative process in which you can receive training, I can't go past my colleague Stacey Barr's 'PuMP Approach to Performance Measurement and KPIs'.[21]

> If your organisation does not have good KPIs, then that is your first job as a risk adviser. Point out the risk and see that they are improved.

Developing KRIs

As Stacey Barr would attest, one could write a book on KPIs. Hers is 100,000 words long. Because KRIs are KPIs, I'm sure you can imagine how much one could learn about them. Assuming you want the cut-down version for now, here I provide my top tips for designing and setting KRIs in your organisation.

KISS

As with everything relating to risk, we must avoid the tendency to make KRIs too complex. I have helped clients develop KRIs, to find the effort that goes into measuring them a real burden. If systems had been in place it would have been different, but they weren't. We should have taken a different approach. In general, I feel the right number for any particular subject, such as your strategic plan, a project or a process, is about five KRIs. Sometimes, one or more of those KRIs may be made up of sub-KRIs. For example, you may have a KRI for customer service. However, it might be a customer service risk index calculated based on four or five sub-KRIs, such as average time to fill an order, max time to fill an order, average time to reply to a customer enquiry and max time to reply to a customer enquiry. You would only do this if, say, 80 per cent of the index was not determined by just one of the sub-KRIs.

> As with everything relating to risk, we must avoid the tendency to make KRIs too complex.

Risk profiles

Whether you are designing KRIs for your strategic objectives or a project or process or anything else, go to your risk profile and identify the key drivers of risk and the key controls on which the management of risk relies. Within the drivers you will find measures that matter. Equally, if key controls are needed to manage a significant risk, then measuring their performance may be critical and hence a KRI can be derived.

Systems

The better your systems, assuming reliable data, the more you can measure and the more you can infer through predictive analytics and machine learning. Once, when I was speaking at a conference for chartered accountants here in Sydney, I asked people to keep their hand in the air if they measured more than 10 KPIs, then 20, 50 and so on. If my memory serves me when I got to 100 there was only one hand up in a room of about 150 people. I asked him how many and he replied 30,000. He was from a media organisation and they were recording everything happening on their website. Hits, hang time, clicking within articles, sharing with friends — you get the drift. My point is that if you have the systems and data governance to do it, you can do some really, really cool and insightful analysis and set up some brilliant early-warning signals.

> Whether you are designing KRIs for your strategic objectives or a project or process or anything else, go to your risk profile and identify the key drivers of risk and the key controls on which the management of risk relies.

Time horizons

My data guru colleague Dr Andrew Pratley has a PhD in Statistics and is Adjunct Lecturer in Business Analytics at the University of Sydney Business School. He has taught me much about measurement in our work with KPIs and KRIs with various clients. A few years ago, when we were touring Australia giving talks on KPIs at various conferences, he introduced me to the Three Horizons of Growth concept introduced by Mehrdad Baghai, Lar Bradshaw, Stephen Coley and David White in their 1999 paper in the *Journal of Business Strategy*.[22] Their thesis was that in order to sustain growth you need to be monitoring which parts of the business are in mature, emergent and embryonic phases, and you need to keep feeding the growth pipeline with new products and services as existing ones fade away.

This led to what I consider some important thinking about strategy and risk over three time horizons that culminated in my development of the strategy funnel in the midst of the COVID-19 pandemic, which I introduce in the next section. In figure 9.2 I show the relationship between strategy and risk over three time horizons. I show the timelines I most commonly find organisations use for their planning. They are one year for executing annual operating plans and managing what is commonly called operational risk; two to five years for strategic planning and strategic risk; and for the last time horizon I use three to thirty years. Three years is highly uncertain for many companies, while the Australian Department of Defence works on thirty-year plans, given it takes more than a decade to develop large strategic assets such as ships and submarines.

The importance of this type of thinking when it comes to KRIs is that for operational risks you are measuring more clearly seen, but not necessarily understood, risks and their controls. So there is a stronger focus for KRIs on controls, whereas strategic risk is more about identifying good lead KPIs to use as KRIs. When it comes to emerging risks, this is much more about reading the signals. And reading signals coming from over the horizon is inherently difficult, which leads nicely into the strategy funnel described in the following pages.

> There is a stronger focus for KRIs on controls, whereas strategic risk is more about identifying good lead KPIs to use as KRIs.

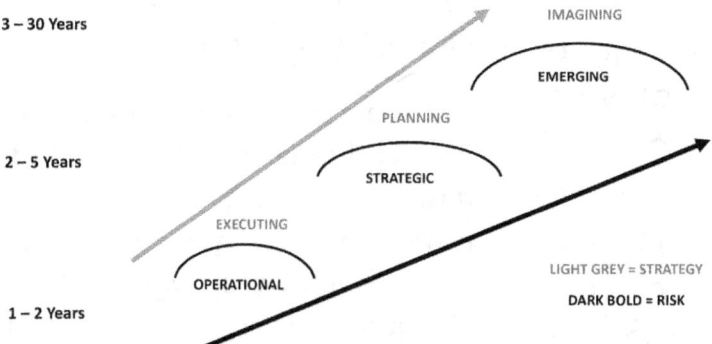

Figure 9.2: The relationship between strategy and risk over three time horizons

The strategy funnel

In developing my strategy funnel concept, I've taken a sales and marketing tool, the sales funnel, and given it a strategic twist. If you are familiar with the sales funnel you will know that prospective customers are moved through or out of the funnel via sales and/or marketing contact points. For example, by clicking on an advertisement they enter the funnel; if they are enticed to fill out an enquiry form for a call from a sales rep they have moved along the funnel; once the sales call has been made and the prospective customer's problem defined they have moved further along, and so on. Sales teams track how many prospective customers are at each stage of the sales funnel because they know their typical attrition rates. For example, for every 100 people that click on an ad, 10 fill out an enquiry form, and of them 7 go on to quotation and on average 5 become customers. So if they are not hitting their numbers at any stage in the funnel, they can seek to diagnose the problem and take action.

> There are many possible futures playing out for your organisation, none of which you can be certain of. The further out in time you look, the more uncertain the view.

The concept of the strategy funnel is illustrated in figure 9.3 and works like this. There are many possible futures playing out for your organisation, none of which you can be certain of. The further out in time you look, the more uncertain the view. Nothing new here. What is your response? Generally, scenario planning and forecasting.

The strategy funnel concept asks you to develop scenarios for your second (Planning) and third (Imagining) time horizons. Once you have them, you do two things.

First and most important is you orientate your strategy to accommodate as many future scenarios as you can with a focus on the ones deemed most likely. Second, you pop them in the top of the funnel. The scenarios built on the furthest time horizons are at the top of the funnel, as they are the ones with greatest uncertainty and greatest variability between good and bad outcomes. The further down in the funnel, the more certainty and the less variability prevails. Now you are able to move the scenarios through the funnel over time by testing the assumptions made or monitoring the outcomes within each scenario.

> First and most important is you orientate your strategy to accommodate as many future scenarios as you can with a focus on the ones deemed most likely. Second, you pop them in the top of the funnel.

In the sales funnel analogy, prospective customers exit the funnel as a lost prospect at any stage of the funnel. In the strategy funnel concept, a scenario exits the funnel or is modified if proven to be way off the mark.

One question that needs answering is 'How many scenarios?' I read once that the answer is four because if you do three, one good, one bad and one in the middle, then management always plans for the middle one. By having four, it forces management to focus more one way or another based on the most likely outcomes. The strategy funnel is different, in that it asks you to develop multiple scenarios at multiple time horizons. How many at each time horizon is a matter of resources. If you are from BHP Billiton, would it be too resource intensive to build four, one at each of the 'planning' and 'imagining' time horizons? If you are a small business operator, you might still do four but with less detail.

Another question that needs answering is 'What criteria do I use to exit a scenario?' How many assumptions or outcomes prove incorrect? The answer is that it is not a case of numbers unless you are doing some sophisticated modelling, which I discuss briefly in the next chapter. You would base it on judgement, just as you used judgement to develop the scenarios in the first place.

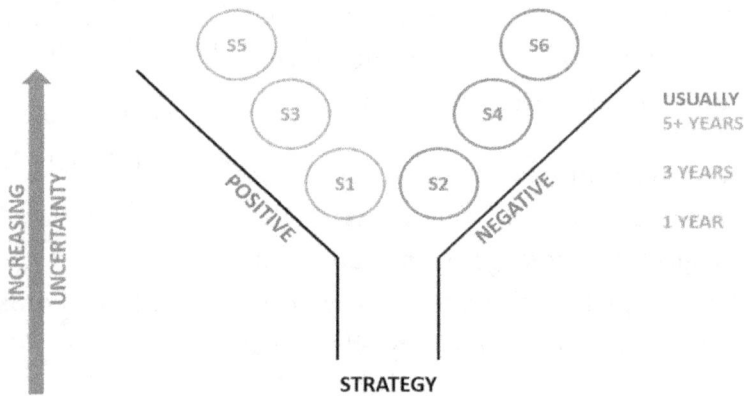

Figure 9.3: The strategy funnel

Do Black Swans send signals?

You have likely heard of 'Black Swans' or 'Black Swan Events' (no, I am not going to refer to them as BSEs). The phrase was coined by Nassim Taleb in his book *The Black Swan: The Impact of the Highly Improbable*.[23] Taleb argues that some things simply cannot be predicted, so don't try. The example he uses is the black swan. Prior to the first visits of non-Indigenous people to the land now known as Australia, there was nothing in the non-Indigenous person's concept of a swan that would lead them to think of a black swan. Why? Because black swans exist only in Australia. So you can well imagine when Dutch explorer Dirk Hartog came upon the west coast of Australia in 1616 that it was highly unlikely he would have turned to his second-in-command and said, 'I bet you a gulden that when we get off this ship we will find a black swan.' The idea would have been ludicrous.

What lessons does Taleb take from this knowledge that, despite what you want to believe, some things can go wrong no matter how well you have planned them? His tip is to always have something in reserve. This type of thinking is a core element of sound risk-based decision making and I like to cover it off with the old saying, 'Remember rule number one!' and for me that is: 'Never bite off

> What lessons does Taleb take from this knowledge that, despite what you want to believe, some things can go wrong no matter how well you have planned them? His tip is to always have something in reserve.

more than you can chew.' I follow this up closely with rule number two, which is: 'Only break rule number one if you have no other choice.' Some risks simply have to be taken if we are to survive.

So do Black Swans send signals? In short, no. If it is a true Black Swan, we would not see it coming. I am near finishing this book in the midst of COVID-19. While some have referred to this pandemic as a Black Swan, many critics I have read agree with me that it is not. We had many, many signals. We had previous outbreaks of a coronavirus that killed many people and was pretty infectious. We had many, many warnings from health practitioners and from politicians. And governments the world over had run disaster scenario exercises with pandemics way worse than COVID-19 is proving.

> I am near finishing this book in the midst of COVID-19. While some have referred to this pandemic as a Black Swan, many critics I have read agree with me that it is not. We had many, many signals.

What about the BP oil spill in the Gulf of Mexico in 2010, another event often referred to as a Black Swan? Were there previous examples of untapped underwater blow-outs of well heads? Yes. Taylor Energy in 2004.[24] Did they have any signals of the devastation that could be caused by a massive oil leak? Yes. *Exxon Valdez* 1989. Did authorities know there was no proven methods of capping a well in deep water? Well, they should have asked the question as there is a multitude of examples of failed safety shut-off systems in the oil and gas industry. So, no, not a Black Swan.

What, then, is a Black Swan? Taleb refers to events like the advent of the world wide web and the 9/11 terrorist attacks on the World Trade Center in 2001. However, he is quick to point out that each depends on the observer. Many in the scientific community predicted something like the internet. As one observer, when I awoke to the news of 9/11 here in Sydney, Australia, the events in front of me were beyond my wildest imagination and so it was a Black Swan. However, later inquiries into 9/11 showed there were clear signals for those in US intelligence that a 9/11-type event was possible.[25] Still, I'm sure the ultimate targets and what happened to those targets were a massive surprise to most in the community.

Again, depending on resources, you should be looking for signals of rare, big positive and negative events. In terms of technology, one source of signals and their interpretation is available from the Future Today Institute (FTI). In fact, the 'Time Cone for Strategic Planning' in their Tech Trends Report 2020 led me to consider their approach alongside my risk over three time horizons, and from there the strategy funnel was born. The

> The FTI approach is to develop identifiable trends from signals as they grow in strength, then to categorise each trend into one of four action quadrants: Act Now, Informs Strategy, Keep Vigilant, Watch and Revisit Later.

FTI approach is to develop identifiable trends from signals as they grow in strength, then to categorise each trend into one of four action quadrants: Act Now, Informs Strategy, Keep Vigilant, Watch and Revisit Later (see figure 9.4). This approach is reflected in how you move scenarios through the strategy funnel.

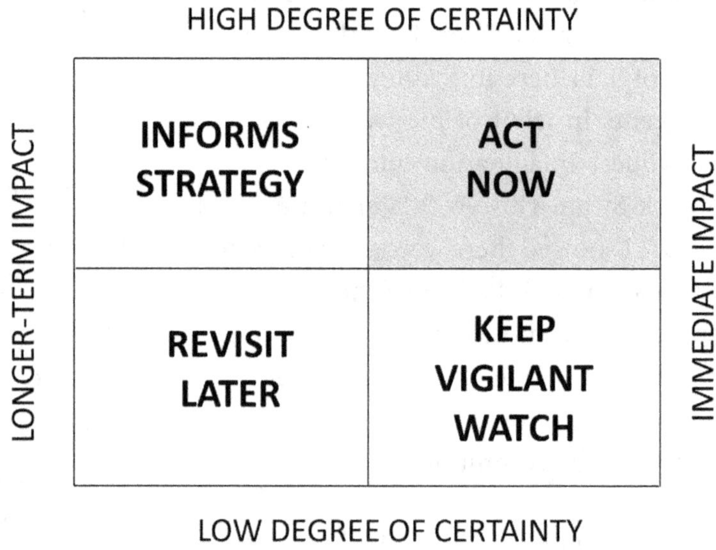

HIGH DEGREE OF CERTAINTY

	INFORMS STRATEGY	ACT NOW	
LONGER-TERM IMPACT	REVISIT LATER	KEEP VIGILANT WATCH	IMMEDIATE IMPACT

LOW DEGREE OF CERTAINTY

Figure 9.4: Future Today Institute's action matrix

Before I leave this chapter, let me explain what I learned about reading the signals during COVID-19.

Planning in pandemics

One key learning from the pandemic is that everyone has a different appetite for risk when it comes to COVID-19.

Naturally most, although not all, people in their seventies and older are more cautious given their higher risk of death if they contract the virus. Similarly, different countries have seen the risk of long-term economic damage of COVID-19 as much higher than the health risk and have accepted higher fatality rates, while countries like New Zealand locked down early and hard. The number one takeaway from this is that you and your organisation need to plan based on your government's strategy. It is not a choice you can make.

> The number one takeaway from this is that you and your organisation need to plan based on your government's strategy. It is not a choice you can make.

Similarly, you cannot choose how your customers might react, whether they hoard your product (toilet paper?) or ban your staff from entering their premises, effectively halting all of your business with them. Nor can you know with certainty when they will change their minds. So the level of uncertainty, as if you needed telling, is extremely high compared to the norm. What this means is the timeline you use for your strategy funnel moves from years to months. Instead of annual review scenario planning for 3–5 and 5–30 years out, it becomes monthly scenario planning for 3–5 and 5–30 months out. There is only one bit of good news from this: you get to find out how good your scenario planning is much sooner than you might otherwise.

Let me suggest as an example an operator of a fine dining group of restaurants using two scenarios at the six months horizon (figure 9.5). At the time of writing there were signs of a second wave of the virus occurring in Australia, and pubs and restaurants were open, but with social distancing restrictions limiting the number of patrons to generally unaffordable levels if not for government wage support.

> The challenge now faced is how you orientate your strategy. Can you devise a way of running your business so it can be profitable under both scenarios?

The challenge now faced is how you orientate your strategy. Can you devise a way of running your business so it can be profitable under both scenarios? For example, can you run a menu set that is cost effective enough, but of sufficient quality, to allow you to charge enough to make a profit? Can you get more efficient in your kitchen so you need fewer staff? Can you centralise some food prep? Can you keep enough cash reserves to outlast your competitors when government support ends and the industry faces the inevitable rationalisation should a vaccine not become available? Can you innovate your business model — for example, by developing an at-home fine dining experience using catering equipment and a team of otherwise unemployed mobile chefs?

9: READING THE SIGNALS | 173

Scenario 1: Good 6-month scenario	Scenario 2: Bad 6-month scenario
The virus: Second wave minimal and controlled. Contact tracing and testing strategy is highly effective. No vaccine available for the foreseeable future.	The virus: Second wave arrived and health authorities lost control initially, but with spring regained control. No vaccine available for the foreseeable future.
Social distancing restrictions: The 4-square-metre restriction capping the number of patrons inside venues is lifted.	Social distancing restrictions: Strict social distancing was reintroduced in July, and pubs and restaurants were closed again through to November 2020.
The government (economy): Direct financial support to pay employees (JobKeeper) is not cut off at end of September. It is phased out via monthly reductions through to 31 December 2020.	The government (economy): Direct financial support to pay employees (JobKeeper) is not cut off at end of September. It is phased out via monthly reductions through to 31 December 2020.
The borders: Interstate borders are fully open. International visitors are welcome but must be tested on arrival and quarantined for 24 hours until test result received.	The borders: Interstate borders between NSW and Victoria are open; all other borders are closed. International visitors remain banned.
The public (economy): The level of spending stays steady through the back end of 2020.	The public (economy): The level of spending returns to June levels by November 2020.
The public (health): The vast majority feel comfortable enough to visit pubs and restaurants.	The public (health): A healthy majority of people return to pubs and clubs by late spring (November).

Figure 9.5: Sample scenarios prepared in June 2020

The answers will of course be different based on the locations and types of clientele you used to have. If you depended on overseas tourists, you will need to add assumptions about whether local tourism will fill the void in full, in part or not at all. Next you work hard on your strategy for one month, doing your best not to second-guess your assumptions unless something major happens. Then revisit the two scenarios at the end of the month. As I wrote when introducing the strategy funnel, the scenarios will change or might be completely jettisoned if your assumptions prove very different from the unfolding reality.

As promised earlier, let's now move on to the topic of quantifying risk.

10

Quantifornication

Plucking numbers out of thin air

The most common form of risk assessment used today involves the subjective (almost always) assignment of a consequence category and a likelihood category, and the use of a risk matrix to arrive at a risk level by 'joining the dots'. *Quantifornication* is my term for the plucking of numbers out of thin air. I see it in business almost every day. *Risk quantifornication* is the plucking of likelihoods and consequences out of thin air for a risk assessment, in particular when trying to estimate really uncertain things. If he were alive today, Bernstein, author of *Against the Gods*, would be dismayed that all the good work of the great mathematicians and economists was going to waste. Remember his last thoughts in the book: 'from FATE and ORIGINAL DESIGN to sophisticated, probability-based forecasts of the future . . .'

In this chapter I explain what the role of risk assessment in decision making should be and how to improve any risk assessment without even worrying about tackling quantifornication. I make the case, with the help of my friend and colleague Dr Andrew Pratley, that defeating quantifornication is much more doable than many risk practitioners think.

The case for good risk assessment

I am often heard to say, 'A bad risk assessment is worse than no risk assessment.' The reason for this is that the human brain is damned good at processing large amounts of information and making enough sense to make informed decisions. We have developed scores and scores of rules of thumb/heuristics that, while imperfect, help us take short-cuts in our decision making. Most are embedded in our genes through thousands and thousands of generations, but we have also developed our own personal ones through decades of experience. And they work well, most of the time.

> We have developed scores and scores of rules of thumb/-heuristics that, while imperfect, help us take short-cuts in our decision making.

We also know, however, through decades of research by the likes of Kahneman and Tversky, that we misfire with heuristics all the time and that sometimes we need to stop and think a little more about a decision. This is where good risk assessment comes in —

where relying on heuristics is potentially dangerous, such as with infrequently made complex decisions.

If you perform a risk assessment poorly, however, a worse situation develops. You head off down a path thinking you know the risks, but you have been misled. You are confident, based on misinformation.

The start of good risk assessment

The international standard on risk management, ISO 31000, tells us that the first step in the risk assessment process is risk identification. Of course it is. If we don't know what the risks are, we can't hope to understand the overall level of risk.

The start of good risk assessment is doing better than thinking about what risks could occur. It is about thinking hard about them. Sure, brainstorming is better than one person thinking about the risks, but there are many more tools you should use to ensure you identify and understand risk.

> The start of good risk assessment is doing better than thinking about what risks could occur.

I have provided examples of my go-to tools in the in the learning resources section of my website bryanwhitefield.com.au/learningresources. They include the Stakeholder, PESTLE and Capability tools I introduced in chapter 7, which I use for establishing context when designing a risk framework. These tools also provide context for risk assessment and good insights into the risks arising because of the stakeholders you need to contend with, the external environment you operate in and the capability of the organisation.

I also learned from Edward de Bono's books on creative thinking that the tools he espoused for creative thinking helped people think outside the box when it comes to identifying risks. Consequently, my other go-to tools are Process Flow Diagram (PFD) and Work Breakdown Structure (WBS), or a variant of a WBS called a Risk Breakdown Structure (RBS). A PFD maps out a process using symbols and lines, so you get a good overall picture of what happens in a certain process. WBSs come from the construction industry and are so named as they break down all the work that needs to happen to deliver the project. A WBS is usually developed based on phases of a project or on functions such as structural and electrical or a combination of phases and functions.

> By focusing in on one element of a PFD or WBS, you think more deeply about them and hence start to identify many more pieces to the puzzle.

PFDs and WBSs use what de Bono called 'focus' to be creative in identifying risks. By focusing in on one element of a PFD or WBS, you think more deeply about them and hence start to identify many more pieces to the puzzle. An RBS is like a WBS but details what could go wrong in a phase of a project or in one of the functions. Again, please see the learning resources section on my website bryanwhitefield.com.au/learningresources for examples.

While using good tools to identify risk is a great start to risk assessment, you also need to consider how you capture the risks identified. Yes, a risk management software application would be great, however, if you don't have software, I have included two MS Excel risk (risk register) templates in the learning resources section of my website bryanwhitefield.com.au/learningresources. One provides greater granularity of risk assessment than the other.

In the more detailed template you will see that I refer to risk statements and two levels of risk. Let me explain. My very strong recommendation is that when you are assessing risk you should always be aligning risks right through to the objectives of the organisation, business unit, team, program, project or activity that is the subject of the risk assessment. And you should prepare a risk statement for each objective and give the objective a risk rating. This facilitates integrated performance and risk reporting which I suggested was essential when explaining my tripartite model of risk management in chapter 7. Knowing the risk level for each objective allows reporting on the progress towards the objective to date AND the risk to future performance.

You will also see in the template that I refer to the risks identified in the risk statement as business risks and the sources of risk for each business risk are also captured. This effectively gives you three levels of depth to your risk identification. While not essential, it can be insightful to go to this level of depth. If you don't need this level, I recommend you use the other template.

I cover risk assessment in more depth in the RMIA ERM course.

Analysing risk

Identifying risk is essential but not enough in itself. You need to know how big a deal all these risks are, what is the sum of the parts, so to speak. And as I mentioned earlier, that is most often done these days using risk criteria and a risk matrix. Many have admirably demonstrated the failings of the risk matrix, none more prominent than Douglas Hubbard in his book *The Failure of Risk Management: Why It's Broken and How to Fix It*. I have been less willing to throw the baby out with the bath water, however. Let me explain.

> Identifying risk is essential but not enough in itself. You need to know how big a deal all these risks are, what is the sum of the parts, so to speak.

In chapter 5 I discussed how the matrix evolved. To settle the argument:

'The risk is high.'

'No it's not!'

Without criteria and a way of combining likelihood and consequence, we only had opinion. The matrix helped decision makers break deadlocks and move forward.

Hubbard and many, many others espouse the use of risk models in place of the misuse of the risk matrix. The use of risk models allows for much more advanced calculation of the combination of likelihood and consequence using probability distributions. The result is the provision of what Hubbard and others call a range estimate for an outcome. That is, instead of being told the likely outcome is a $5 million loss, the decision maker is provided with information that suggests the loss could be between, say, $4.2 million and $12 million, along with an estimate of the likelihood that it will exceed $4.2 million and not exceed $12 million within a certain statistical confidence interval of, say, 90 or 95 per cent. That is, only in unusual circumstances will the loss be less than $4.2 million or more than $12 million. Having this sort of information affects decision making. No longer are decision makers fixated on the most likely outcome, which of course will rarely occur as it is just one point on a continuum from $4.2 million to $12 million.

Most organisations do not go down the path of sophisticated risk modelling for any one, or combination, of reasons, such as:

1. The belief that what they are currently doing is good or good enough.
2. Risk modelling is too expensive and takes too long.
3. The cost and time don't outweigh the benefits.
4. A lack of data.

Hubbard nicely counters all these concepts in his numerous books on decision making under uncertainty. However, in my experience the problem is an unspoken one. Most people don't have the confidence. They don't know where

> Most people don't have the confidence. They don't know where to start. They don't know how to even explain to decision makers what it means to develop a risk model. That's not their fault.

to start. They don't know how to even explain to decision makers what it means to develop a risk model. That's not their fault. The risk profession has not spent a lot of time on helping them find the confidence. And that's where my colleague Dr Andrew Pratley and I step in.

Quantifying risk

As I was putting the finishing touches on this book, Andrew and I were preparing a series of blogs for risk practitioners to help those not ready to advance to risk modelling to start the journey. To get more accurate estimates of likelihood and/or consequence and/or the cost-benefit of investing in controls to manage them. And to build their confidence so they could progress to risk modelling in their own good time. Following are Andrew's ideas relating statistical concepts to risk management in support of my quest to defeat quantifornication.

Accuracy over buckshot

Buckshot follows the scatter-gun approach: fire the shot knowing that, most likely, some of it will hit the target. It's what we do when we 'quantifornicate'. Not a great strategy when making decisions under uncertainty. Better would be to have more accurate estimates.

Let's use the example of cyber security. How much cyber security is enough? There are two broad extremes that are worth starting from: do nothing, spend no money and hope for the best; or do everything, have an unlimited budget and know you're safe. The value of extreme positions is not to advocate for one or the other but to place markers. The current theory is that the more you spend, the more you can do and therefore the safer you are.

> There are two broad extremes that are worth starting from: do nothing, spend no money and hope for the best; or do everything, have an unlimited budget and know you're safe.

Let's test this out. If you had a house with ten entrances and you could spend money to secure only seven of these, in theory you'd be safer than someone who could secure only three of the entrances. This statement is true only if you assume that every entrance is equally likely to be used in a break-in. This assumption is rarely true, even when it seems entirely reasonable. Another example of this idea is presented as the Monty Hall problem:

Suppose you're on a game show, and you're given the choice of three doors. Behind one door is a car; behind the others, goats. You pick a door, say number 1, and the host, who knows what's behind the doors, opens another door, say number 3, which has a goat. He then says to you, 'Do you want to pick door No. 2?' Is it to your advantage to switch your choice?

When presented with this seemingly straightforward problem, the vast majority of people choose to keep their selection — and they end up disappointed and go home with a goat. If you were to change your pick, though, you would have a 66 per cent chance of winning. As nicely spelled out in a blog by Jim Frost, an excerpt from which I have provided below.[26]

It turns out that there are only nine different combinations of choices and outcomes. Therefore, I can just show them all to you and we calculate the percentage for each outcome.

You Pick	Prize Door	Don't Switch	Switch
1	1	Win	Lose
1	2	Lose	Win
1	3	Lose	Win
2	1	Lose	Win
2	2	Win	Lose
2	3	Lose	Win
3	1	Lose	Win
3	2	Lose	Win
3	3	Win	Lose
		3 Wins (33%)	**6 Wins (66%)**

Andrew's and my message to you is that not everything is what it seems. We often need to look beyond what we see and ask ourselves if the underlying assumptions we are making are reasonable. By doing this we can start to make more accurate assessments.

The danger of the guessing game

We're far better at identifying good and bad writing than we are identifying good and bad numbers. The premise of this idea almost doesn't seem logical. How can a language like English, with all of its oddities, be easier when separating the good from the bad?

> We're far better at identifying good and bad writing than we are identifying good and bad numbers.

Our education in English has a substantial amount of time devoted to comparing different types of writing and methods to improve readability and comprehension. We accept and understand there is no 'right way' and don't become fixated on this idea. Almost all of our number education focuses on calculations to get the right answer. We rarely discuss where the numbers come from, or their validity.

> Almost all of our number education focuses on calculations to get the right answer. We rarely discuss where the numbers come from, or their validity.

When we talk about numbers we tend to assume we're discussing clear and agreeable ideas, such as the temperature in a room (19°C), our height without shoes (1,820 mm) or the number of customers that visit the store in a day (65). These are fairly easy to check. In the same way, as each of these three scenarios generates a specific value, we can generate specific values for the predicted maximum temperature tomorrow, the predicted height of a child when they turn 18 or the number of customers we think will make a purchase tomorrow.

While we inherently know that the 'weatherman' is not always right, and that the height of a child and the number of buyers are only predictions, it is how we treat this information that is important. In some instances, we will treat the information with caution. Some of us will take something warm in case the temperature is a few degrees cooler than predicted. And for something like the height of a child, the timeline for realisation of that prediction is so far out, we give it little consideration — just as many people treat climate change. And for the number of customers we think will make a purchase tomorrow, we make decisions on staffing and inventory.

> The reality is that many of the important decisions we make every day are based on guesstimates that we like to believe are true values — that is, the truth!

This last illustration of customers is an example of how we tend to intermix reliable numbers (the measured number of customers in the store) with what are normally unreliable numbers (the estimated number of customers purchasing). While temperature estimates are based on sophisticated modelling with set margins of error, the estimate of customer purchases is usually an educated guess, unless you work for a company that has invested in analytics *and* run the numbers with statistical validity.

The reality is that many of the important decisions we make every day are based on guesstimates that we like to believe are true values — that is, the truth!

From guestimate to estimate — as simple as 1, 2, 3

Most people who have had to sit through an entire class of statistics might reasonably assume the staff are sadistic and enjoy seeing people fall asleep, and slowly stop turning up. If you met the staff outside of this context, you'd never pick them to teach this subject. Like most educators, they're passionate and spend considerable time and effort trying to explain the ideas.

Why do so many educators in statistics consistently fail to translate these ideas into something that people can both remember and use? The problem is the language, not the numbers. Part of the problem with statistics, as is the case with most technical subjects, is the unique terminology.

> Part of the problem with statistics, as is the case with most technical subjects, is the unique terminology.

While there is a learning curve to the terminology, most of us are left with a dizzying array of formulas, methods and tables to work out how to use. None of which make sense outside of a specific context. So let us help you.

The field of statistics boils down to providing answers to one of three types of questions:

1. Questions about probability.
2. Questions about differences.
3. Questions about relationships.

Applying this three-question framework in risk is easiest seen through the risk matrix. We all know the shortcomings of the technique, but how do we use statistics to improve our ability to make decisions? The risk matrix has two axes — likelihood and consequence — and a third aspect, control measures to affect likelihood or consequence.

Using the three-question framework we could link:

1. Questions about probability to the likelihood axis.

    For example, we could use the method of probability to improve our estimate of the likelihood of a successful cyber-attack. To do this we might use the binomial distribution to model the number of active threats.

2. Questions about differences to control measures.

    We could use the method of differences to determine if one control measure is more effective than another. To do this we might run a two-sample t-test comparing a spam filter to a compulsory online learning module.

3. Questions about relationships to any of (i) likelihood & consequence (ii) likelihood & control measures or (iii) consequence & control measures.

We could use the method of relationships to determine if there is a relationship between control measures and likelihood. To do this we might run a regression analysis to see if spending more money on control measures actually reduces the likelihood of the risk occurring.

> The risk matrix has two axes — likelihood and consequence — and a third aspect, control measures to affect likelihood or consequence.

Bonus: Andrew and I recorded three videos, one each for the three types of questions and applied them to controls for the RMIA and AISA Risk and Cyber 2020 conference. You can view them via my learning resources page at bryanwhitefield.com.au/learningresources.

Taste testing quantification

The story of statistics started with a question about differences. In 1935 R.A. Fisher set out to test if someone really could taste the difference between tea where the milk was poured in before or after the tea. Fisher's experimental design was simple. Eight cups of tea were prepared, four

> The opportunity for professionals like you is to develop the ability to see situations and identify how statistical methods can be used.

with the milk poured before, four with the milk poured after. Four were presented to Muriel Bristol in a random order. The lady correctly identified all four cups and Fisher came up with the mathematics to show that this result was extremely unlikely to occur by chance. The mathematics behind this became known as Fisher's exact test.

Fisher went on to study crops and provided the framework for much of what we use today. The questions Fisher answered were related to many of the questions we're interested in today. For example:

- Would one type of fertiliser promote faster crop growth than another?
- Did the way the crops were planted impact their growth?
- Would the amount of water provided change the yield?

Based on the answers to these questions, Fisher was able to determine how to make the best decisions, when choices are available, based on statistical analysis.

All business leaders make decisions between different approaches. Critically, and fortunately for us, we don't need to be capable of developing statistical methods like Fisher, we just need to be able to apply them. While Fisher used pencil, pad and slide-rule, business leaders today have access to 90 years of research and development that are pretty well captured in Microsoft Excel.

The opportunity for professionals like you is to develop the ability to see situations and identify how statistical methods can be used. We tend to think statistics apply only to large data sets full of numbers. As the example at the start showed, Fisher was able to test if someone could tell the difference in how tea was prepared. Which informs people on how best to make tea for those who like the taste with the milk poured before or after. Fisher accomplished this without collecting a single number.

The questions you answer on differences could well be more profound and important than how to pour tea to your liking (unless you *really* like tea), but the underlying principle is the same. Statistical analysis doesn't have to be something relegated to the too hard basket in favour of other less accurate methods.

> To ensure you become confident, you can help senior executives make better decisions with *your data*, not big data.

The scope of this book does not allow for a deeper lesson in applied statistics. And rather than provide you with some resources on my website that may actually be more confronting than helpful, Andrew and I have prepared a training program specifically designed for you. To ensure

> A mindset that pushes you to seek out the right data, often at your fingertips, and to learn just enough about Microsoft Excel to use the tools developed by mathematicians over the last 90 years to provide decision makers with real insight.

you become confident, you can help senior executives make better decisions with *your data*, not big data.

It's about your data, not big data

With the above examples I hope we have been able to show you that our reliance on guestimates must be improved and that we have demonstrated that it might not be as hard as you think to do so. You don't need bucket loads of big data, you just need a data mindset. A mindset that pushes you to seek out the right data, often at your fingertips, and to learn just enough about Microsoft Excel to use the tools developed by mathematicians over the last 90 years to provide decision makers with real insight. So that you have accuracy over buckshot.

11

The pathways to success!

Risk-based decision making

In the final chapter I will discuss the ultimate skill you will need to help you be successful: the power of persuasion. Before I do so, in this penultimate chapter I want to show you the pathways you may need to take to reach the point where you can say to yourself, 'I believe I have done it. Success!'

> I want to show you the pathways you may need to take to reach the point where you can say to yourself, 'I believe I have done it. Success!'

'Risk-based decision making', at first glance, seems a pretty straightforward idea. A decision maker who weighs the pros and cons of a decision before making it. It only takes a moment's thought to see how complex it really is. How likely are the pros? How likely are the cons? Could the pros or the cons be much greater or worse than I have first considered? Now ponder these issues further.

What might influence me when identifying and assessing the pros and cons? Do I lack knowledge? Where and from whom might I derive this knowledge? Will I listen to the right people? What will I hear and what will fall on deaf ears? How might my unconscious biases ultimately affect me?

> How far and wide should my research extend when I consider the pros and cons?

How far and wide should my research extend when I consider the pros and cons? Does my world stop at the front door of the building? Does it extend to my customers, beyond a simple 'take it or leave it' equation? What obligation do I have to investors? And what of the general public? Do I consider some of the public more or less than others in my decision making? If you are a politician or government official, you will have very broad responsibilities. The prime minister or president of a nation is, or should be, taking into account all of the population when making decisions of national interest. Decisions like where the budget is allocated and whether the budget needs to be in the black or whether and when a deficit may be legitimate. These considerations extend beyond national boundaries, which is why wealthier countries come to the aid of other countries when crisis hits. Why? To pursue our national interests, yes, but also to honour — to live — our values.

I started this book with a description of risk management through recent decades and a view of risk management in the 2020s, the decade of accountability, influence and risk leadership. I suggested that business leaders will be applying risk-based decision making as they choose what risks to take and which not to. I proposed that by following risk-based decision making they will be aware of and managing their unconscious bias. And I expressed the need for leaders who are true to organisational values. But how to get them there?

The pathways

When I think about strong risk leadership in an organisation, I think of strong risk leaders working alongside strong business leaders, each leading alongside the other, the business leader taking the risks and the risk leader helping them to think through their decisions. Unfortunately, I rarely hear about this, let alone see it. One reason is that I work with organisations that need help because they are not at the top of their game. The other is, I believe, because it is rarely found. I am often asked which company in Australia does

> When I think about strong risk leadership in an organisation, I think of strong risk leaders working alongside strong business leaders, each leading alongside the other, the business leader taking the risks and the risk leader helping them to think through their decisions.

it best. I don't have a good answer. The answer I often give is Macquarie Group, but even they have been subject to both negative press and the influence of regulation that distorts risk advising and risk-taking. Let me explain.

There are lots of organisations in Australia making plenty of money that one could place on a pedestal for one reason or another but that fail when it comes to risk leadership. As I noted in the introduction, BHP Billiton has made shareholders plenty of money. In the five years from January 2011 to late 2015 its average share price was above $30. In November 2015 the Mariana mine disaster hit and the share price fell to a low of about $15 in January 2016. It took them most of 2016 to recover the ground lost. Since then they have implemented a risk transformation project and their share price has climbed steadily. When I have spoken to risk leaders within the company, however, they have dared not claim they have reached the pinnacle of success. Anthony Reardon, from BHP, was the RMIA Risk Manager of the Year in 2018, in no small part because of his work on the transformation he helped lead. However, during the talks he gave to the RMIA chapters across the country, he left no one in any doubt about how much work was left to be done.

> There are lots of organisations in Australia making plenty of money that one could place on a pedestal for one reason or another but that fail when it comes to risk leadership.

Then there are the banks. They make a lot of money. And

while the Royal Commission in Australia has hurt Australian banks, it is only a speed bump along their profit highway. Yet the evidence of the failings of executives, unmoved by the influence of the risk professionals in the organisation, is superlatively documented in the APRA report into the CBA and in the transcripts and final report of the Royal Commission.

But what of Macquarie Group? They fared well at the Royal Commission yet they too have had their scandals, as headlined by *The New Daily* in May 2018, the *Financial Review* in July 2018 and *Small Caps* in November 2018.[27] The *Small Caps* article highlights one of Macquarie's greatest strengths. They hold their senior decision-makers to account. While the larger banks pay bigger base salaries and smaller bonuses, Macquarie pay smaller base salaries and large bonuses. Another difference: while the large banks can't claw back bonuses, Macquarie pays out bonuses over a number of years. And, you guessed it, bonuses can be adjusted if there are problems with profit or with the regulator.

Macquarie's strength in holding executives accountable is not the only reason I hold them out as one of the shining lights. For many, many years they have had a risk function that asks the hard questions. Executives cannot simply make a call. They have hoops to jump through. In the vernacular of the Three Lines Model of risk management, they provide plenty of challenge.

Why my reluctance then to crown Macquarie as the golden

child of how risk should play out? One reason is obviously that they are not scandal-free. Another is I simply don't know as I have not worked with them. A third reason is uncertainty as to what will happen in Macquarie bank given the new demands of regulators post the Royal Commission. Remember my comments on the influence of regulators:

> *Regulators demand red tape. The risk function creates the red tape. And the business spends the rest of the time trying to avoid the red tape.*

Here we have successful companies like BHP and Macquarie that are good at risk management but evidently are not fully there yet. What, then, of the pathways? Refer to figure 11.1.

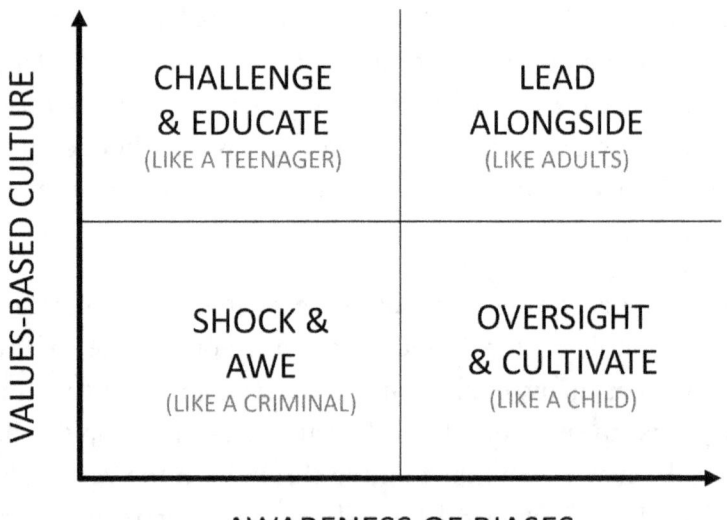

Figure 11.1: Risk leadership

Leading alongside

The pinnacle of success is represented at the top right of the diagram, where risk leaders lead alongside business leaders. Like an adult friend advising on a decision, it is when business leaders work with risk leaders to ensure they are making decisions in full consideration of organisational values and having done their best to overcome their unconscious biases. If you are not there with your leadership team, then you will be starting from one of the other quadrants. Each requires a different approach.

Shock and Awe

If your organisation has leaders who are consistently making decisions that do not conform with your organisation's declared values and who lack awareness of the unconscious biases that affect their decision making, then your job will be a tough one. Some shock and awe will be required — shocks, hopefully, you can generate through strong analysis and personal influence, not by waiting for organisational calamities. I use the analogy 'Like a Criminal', though I recognise that for most it is over the top. Yet executives have been sent to jail and plenty more have been lucky not to be. If you are at all familiar with police tactics, they will often use shock and awe with

> If your organisation has leaders who are consistently making decisions that do not conform with your organisation's declared values, then your job will be a tough one.

people who come into contact with them for the first time for the wrong reasons. It is about 'heading them off at the pass' to reduce the likelihood of future crime.

Oversight and Cultivate

A little easier is when your leaders are in the main, aware of their unconscious biases and are letting themselves down by not living true to organisational values. Here the board or senior executive will need you to provide oversight with close support until you and they are able to cultivate a strong, values-based culture. You must use your influencing skills to remind leaders constantly how their decisions align or fail to align with the organisation's values. But here is a tip. No one, but no one on the planet, likes to be 'oversighted'. So call it something else. Maybe express your role as custodians of all stakeholders helping to seek a balance between customer, regulation and profit. By all means provide the oversight the board needs, just don't call it that!

> You must use your influencing skills to remind leaders constantly how their decisions align or fail to align with the organisation's values.

Challenge and Educate

Similar but different is when your leaders are doing their best to fulfil the organisational purpose while holding true to the organisation's values, but lack awareness of their unconscious biases. Here the board or senior executive will need you to use your influencing skills to subtly challenge decisions where you see fit. More importantly, your role is to educate them about bias. And another tip. People often say they like to be challenged by their direct reports or by internal advisers. However, as already noted, most people like to be challenged only when they are proven right! Again, call it something else. Perhaps compare your role to that of the insights team from marketing, only you are providing insights across the whole breadth of their decision-making landscape.

> People often say they like to be challenged by their direct reports or by internal advisers. However, as already noted, most people like to be challenged only when they are proven right!

There you have it. There are three pathways to success for you and your organisation. One is tackling unconscious bias. Another is shifting and instilling strong organisational values in decision making. The third is standing with one foot on each path and hurtling your way up the middle. All are challenging. All need the gift of influence. The power of persuasion. Which is the subject of the final chapter.

12

Persuasive advising

Shifting mountains

Reaching the pinnacle of our profession, where you are leading alongside the business leaders you serve, should not be underestimated. Given the brick walls and the seemingly immovable mountains of single-minded, closed-minded, even ill-minded executives you have had to persuade and conciliate, you probably don't underestimate it. How much more evidence do we need beyond what has been produced by the likes of Kahneman, Tversky, Thaler, Gigerenzer, Nutt, Ariely and Taleb? All have shown the weaknesses in our decision making. Yet I still hear this type of thinking from senior executives. Take, for example, these two observations from a casual conversation I once had with a CFO:

> Breath 1: 'You know, auditors come and look at the books over a couple of weeks but they have no real idea of what's

going on. They think they do, but no, they only know what management let them know.'

Breath 2: 'If I had more time, I'm sure I could do well picking winners on the stock market.'

Do you see the irreconcilability of these two propositions? One is that no one outside the organisation really knows what is going on inside listed and externally audited companies. The other is you can pick which listed and externally audited company will outperform the market. Sure, you might pick a winner in a company that is living true to its values, but then you might not, given that even the auditors 'have no real idea of what's going on'.

> You might pick a winner in a company that is living true to its values, but then you might not, given that even the auditors 'have no real idea of what's going on'.

Take Leighton Holdings, for example. CEO Wal King was a hero in the industry and in Australian business generally, having won multiple industry awards and the Order of Australia in 2004. He was CEO of Leightons from 1987 until the end of 2010. Within 12 months of his departure Leightons had announced more than $1.1 billion in write-downs. A drop in the share price ensued, followed by a class action. Next the new CEO, David Stewart, who had been in the business for years, resigned. It did not end there. Cue an Australian Federal Police (AFP) investigation into bribery scandals, more troubled projects, fines by the regulator ASIC relating to market disclosures and a billion-dollar problem in their Middle East operations.

And now the clanger for the risk profession. In 2008 the RMIA Risk Manager of the Year was David Hudson, from Leighton Holdings. In 2008 I was the NSW Chapter President for the RMIA and hosted a lunch for 114 to hear Hudson's story. It was compelling. I well understood why he won the award. He had previously been the head of one of the business units of Leightons. He truly understood the business. He could talk their language. He knew the challenges and the ways to get things done. Yet during 2008 and in the years either side, the seeds of the problems in 2011 were sown. It's a tough job to shift mountains.

Shifting values

I have mentioned that many scholars have pointed out our fallibility as decision makers. While unconscious bias is key, there is no doubt in my mind that our values are a key driver of our biases. Think racism, sexism, elitism and plenty of other isms. Isms are expressions of values, most of them nothing to be proud of. To shift the mountain we must challenge isms, and that means shifting values.

> While unconscious bias is key, there is no doubt in my mind that our values are a key driver of our biases.

Do you think we can shift our values? Yes, we can. As Amy

Webb from the Future Today Institute says in her book *The Big Nine* about the rise of artificial intelligence, 'Our cherished beliefs are in constant flux.' She cites the shift from torrid politicking to implicit permission for 'national leaders to hurl offensive, hate-filled social media posts at each other and for pundits to spew polarizing, incendiary commentary on video, in blog posts, and even in traditional news publications. It's nearly impossible now to imagine the discretion and respect for privacy during FDR's presidency, when the press took great care never to mention or show his paralysis.'

> Amy Webb makes the point that for AI to make decisions for us, it needs to understand our values.

She makes the point that for AI to make decisions for us, it needs to understand our values. 'Building AI means predicting the values of the future. Our values aren't static. So how do we teach machines to reflect our values without influencing them? Yet our values shift over time. So how do we design AI for shifting values?'

Another day I will solve the problem of AI. For now I want only to convince you that shifting people's values is possible, even in the most difficult of circumstances. My friend and colleague Cathy Burke was CEO of The Hunger Project. In her book *Unlikely Leaders*, she writes of the unbelievable work she and her colleagues did in places like Bangladesh to lift people out of poverty and ward off starvation through the creation of women leaders in local villages. One story she tells is of Ishita, a 12-year-old Bangladeshi girl whose likely destiny was to be sold into prostitution and sex slavery as a consequence of traditional customs around dowries that ruined so many poor families.

When Cathy and her co-workers came to Ishita's village, local people were invited to information sessions and mobilised to spread the word, door to door, of the truth about the fate of the girls who were sold across the border in India. They were also trained to teach the village that girls were 'an asset worth investing in'. By the time Cathy returned eight years later, the practice had stopped, and young men she spoke with were offended when she asked them if they would take dowry payments.

Shifting gears

In chapter 6 I discussed risk leadership in the context of moving from risk as a compliance activity and a drag on the organisation to risk as the key to sustainable growth. I also showed that being a behaviour changer was evidence that your influence had increased significantly. Now I want to see you shift up a gear in order to become a trusted adviser (as shown in figure 12.1). How do you know you have succeeded as a senior risk leader in your organisation? The first question to ask yourself is, 'When does the CEO ask for your advice?' If the answer is, 'Well before the decision is made,' then you are likely a

> How do you know you have succeeded as a senior risk leader in your organisation?

trusted adviser. If the answer is, 'After the decision is made,' meaning they are throwing it over the fence to you to do the 'risk bits' or to see if you can find fault (like you usually do), you still have some work to do.

Here is the secret to becoming a trusted adviser. You must first learn to persuade. You must persuade those you need to influence to take your advice, so they learn to trust you.

How do I know this? When I was the RMIA NSW Chapter President organising education events, the number one question I was asked was, 'How do I get the CEO to listen to me?' Throughout the six years I was president, the question never changed. And here we are in 2020 and the same question is still being asked by risk professionals, only quietly or only in their heads. Why? Because time and again risk professionals find solace in policy, frameworks and systems, where they can do their technical work. And have near-zero impact on decision making in the business.

If you want to make the impact you know you can, you must become a persuasive adviser so you can become a trusted adviser. To become a persuasive adviser, you need to stand in the shoes of those you serve and align your advice with their needs and wants. If you can do this and communicate your advice in a compelling way, you will gain their trust, and your partnership will shift gears.

Persuasive Adviser: How to Turn Red Tape Into Blue Ribbon is the subject of another of my books. I encourage you to grab a copy! Link to the book is: https://www.bryanwhitefield.com.au/product/persuasive-advising-book/

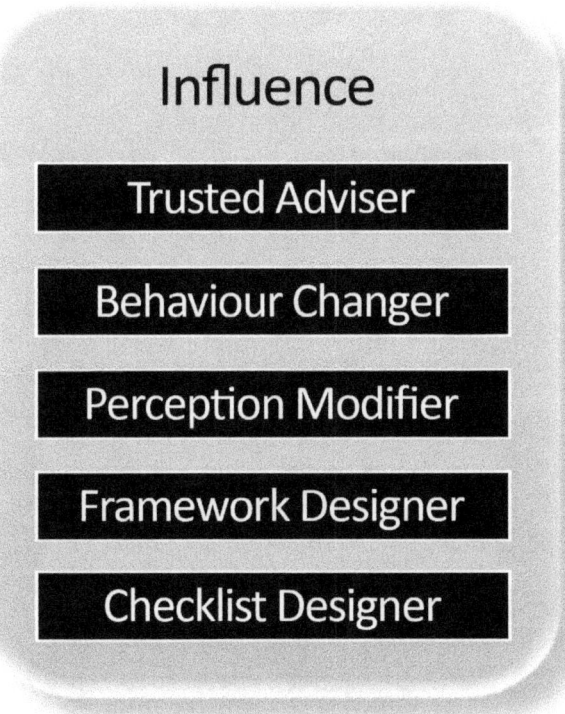

Figure 12.1: The influence ladder

The wrap

I am passionate about

I am passionate about risk. I want people to succeed with minimal unintended impact. While I feel I should have written this book a long time ago, I take comfort in knowing that it is a better book and will help more people in the field of risk management because of what I have learned since even thinking about writing my first book.

My greatest opportunity to make a difference on this planet was presented to me in late 2018 when the Risk Management Institute of Australasia (RMIA) asked me to design and run their flagship training program, Enterprise Risk Management. I could see the opportunity. The chance to share the knowledge I had accrued from over 30 years in the field of risk with many hundreds of risk professionals of all kinds, who would in turn go on to influence decision makers across every sector of the economy.

I took up the challenge with gusto and developed a two-day program using the 'flipped classroom' approach. The first day focuses on online, self-paced learning. On the second day I share my tips and tricks from my 30-plus years of experience.

After I ran the first program, in June 2019, I knew I needed to write this book. While I could impart a lot of knowledge in a two-day program, there was so much more I wanted to say. To give to the profession. And here it is. My gift to you. And if we have not had the pleasure of meeting, I hope we can one day soon. Perhaps in the Enterprise Risk Management course I run for the RMIA, where you can explore first-hand the concepts outlined in this book with me and a cohort of like-minded risk professionals.

Endnotes

1   https://www.psychologytoday.com/ca/blog/beyond-the-doubt/200910/the-uncertainty-paradox?amp. Accessed 21 July 2019.

2   Hoyt, Robert E., and Liebenberg, Andrew P. 'Evidence of the Value of Enterprise Risk Management', *Journal of Applied Corporate Finance*, vol. 27, no. 1, Winter 2015.

3   Lechner, Philipp, and Gatzert, Nadine. 'Determinants and Value of Enterprise Risk Management: Empirical Evidence from Germany', *European Journal of Finance*, vol. 24, no. 10, 2018.

4[4] Rob van der Meulen, 'COVID-19 Makes a Strong Business Case for Enterprise Risk Management', April 10, 2020. https://www.gartner.com.

5   Bernstein, Peter L. *Against the Gods: The Remarkable Story of Risk*, John Wiley & Sons, 1996, 1998, p. 337.

6   Lovallo, D., and Sibony, O. 'The Case for Behavioural Strategy', *McKinsey Quarterly*, March 2010.

7   https://www.psychologytoday.com/au/basics/groupthink. Accessed 19 July 2020.

8   Janis, Irving L. 'Groupthink and Group Dynamics: A Social Psychological Analysis of Defective Policy

Decisions', *Policy Studies Journal*, vol. 2, no. 1, September 1, 1973.

9   Dignan, Aaron. 'Changing Organisational Mindset', *Stanford Social Innovation Review*, March 18, 2019. https://ssir.org/books/excerpts/entry/changing_organizational_mindset

10 'Bupa's aged care homes failing standards across Australia', ABC 7:30 Report, by Anne Connolly and John Stewart, 12 September 2019, https://www.abc.net.au/news/2019-09-12/bupas-aged-care-homes-failing-standards-across-australia/11501050

11 I named the town only because I love that name! It comes from watching too many Bugs Bunny shows, and if you don't know what I mean, you probably don't know the relationship between a cassette tape and a pencil. My thanks to one of my mentors, Matt Church, for that last line!

12 https://www.abc.net.au/news/2019-09-12/bupas-aged-care-homes-failing-standards-across-australia/11501050, 12 September 2019

13 Heric, Michael, Cichocki, Paul, Qadir, Adnan, and Stumbles, Peter. 'Break out from the G&A cost treadmill: How support functions can delight their customers, not just cut costs. Bain and Co., 2013.

14 Ibid.

15 Barrett, Pat. 'Managing Risk: Perspectives from the ANAO'. Address to COMNET — Canberra, November 27, 1996.

16 Martens, Frank, & Rittenberg, Larry. 'Risk Appetite — Critical to Success, COSO, May 2020.

17 https://www.oldest.org/technology/companies/

18 https://image-src.bcg.com/Images/BCG-Die-Another-Day-Dec-2015%20rev_tcm9-168290.pdf

19 https://waitbutwhy.com/2015/01/artificial-intelligence-revolution-1.html

20 V.F. Ridgway. 'Dysfunctional Consequences of Performance Measurements', *Administrative Science Quarterly*, vol. 1, no. 2, September 1956, pp. 240–7.

21 https://www.staceybarr.com/about/pump/

22 Based on Baghai, M., Bradshaw, L., Coley, S., and White, D. 'Performance measures Calibrating for Growth', *Journal of Business Strategy*, vol. 20, no. 4, 17–21, 1999.

23 Nassim Nicholas Taleb. *The Black Swan: The Impact of the Highly Improbable*, 2007, Random House, New York.

24 https://www.theguardian.com/commentisfree/2018/dec/28/worst-oil-disaster-youve-never-heard-of-taylor-energy-gulf-of-mexico

25 Many in the intelligence community in the US may have warned of similar events to 9/11.

26 Jim Frost, 'The Monty Hall Problem: A Statistical Illusion', https://statisticsbyjim.com/fun/monty-hall-problem/

27 https://thenewdaily.com.au/finance/finance-news/2018/05/04/macquarie-dodged-royal-commission/

https://www.afr.com/companies/financial-services/how-macquarie-has-so-far-avoided-a-roasting-at-the-banking-royal-commission-20180701-h123t2

https://smallcaps.com.au/macquarie-royal-commission-example-big-banks-follow/

www.ingramcontent.com/pod-product-compliance
Lightning Source LLC
Chambersburg PA
CBHW070422010526
44118CB00014B/1860